BACK TO THE TABLE

ISBN 0-7868-6854-6

First Edition

10 9 8 7 6 5 4 3 2

BACK TO THE TABLE

The Reunion of Food and Family

ART SMITH

New York

This book has evolved through the contributions of many people. I wish to thank:

Book Team

Wendy Graham – Executive Project Manager
Jesus Salgueiro – Artistic Director
Karen Armijo – Chef/Executive Assistant
  to Art Smith
Domenica Catelli – Assistant Recipe Developer
Sheron Leonard – Writing consultant
  to Art Smith
Marisa Molinaro – Production Coordinator
  and Location Scout

Project Support

Lisa Halliday – Director of Corporate and
  Media Relations, Harpo Entertainment Group
Thalia Kalodimos – Art Director/Special Projects
  Producer, Harpo Productions

Book Design

Grady, Campbell Inc.
Kerry Grady – Principal Designer
Don Campbell – Principal
Tracy Jenkins, Kayo Takasugi, and
Mark Stammers – Designers

Color Food Photography

Dave Jordano – Photographer
Bill Huber – Photo Assistant
Jeannette Jordano – Assistant Stylist
Josephine Orba – Food Stylist
Susie Skoog – Assistant Food Stylist
Karen Johnson – Prop Stylist
Marena Upton – Studio Manager

Black and White Photography

Paul Elledge – Photographer
Leasha Overturf – Producer
Nate Eldridge – Assistant
Audra Daniliauskas – Studio Manager

Darcy McGrath – Make-up and Hair

Dedication

This book would have not been possible without the love of the many great women in my life.

Thank you Mother, Addie Mae; Grandmother Georgia; Grandmother Mabel; and Leila Curry. Thank you Evelyn, Lois, Diane, Brenda, Annette, Millicent, Wanda, Mrs. Noblejas, Mrs. Tomlinson, Rainey, Mrs. Graham, Gwen, Cissy, Suzanne, Kendall, Annella, Mary Jane, Margie, Annie B, Julie, Carolyn, Rachel, Cathy, Sylvia, Fredda, Mrs. Silverman, Edna, Marion, Mrs. Gray, Shelley, Mrs. Chapman, Malou, Mrs. McNally, Karen, Domenica, Mary, Marilyn, Mrs. Crowe, Mrs. Block, Madge, Darcy, Wendy K., Tamara, Martha, Alexis, Patricia, Lisa, Jill, Mrs. Simmons, Sheron, Sue, Debbie, Libby, Anita, Kelly, Angelique, Ina, Marisa, Wendy, Renée, Louise, Dianne, Ms. King, Mrs. E. for all your love and support.

A special thank you to Ms. Oprah Winfrey and Mr. Stedman Graham. Thank you for inviting me to your table and giving me this wonderful opportunity to share my life's work with the families of the world.

Contents

List of Recipes

Back to the Table

The table has always served as a symbol of congregation, the place where we celebrate our loved ones through the generations-old tradition of sharing a meal.

Dining together allows us to better understand who we are, regardless of our social status. The food does not have to be elegant, complicated, or fancy. I find that busy people like simple food – the busier they are, the simpler the food. None of the recipes in this book are difficult; most are straightforward, down-home Southern food with a few more contemporary dishes.

Getting back to the table allows us to love and nurture each other and renew connections to our families – however they may be configured in this diverse and ever-changing society. Such connections are crucial in a fast-paced world where we feel more disconnected every day. One of the best ways I know to restore that daily balance is to sit down at the table.

As a child growing up in rural Florida, I learned the importance of the family table. It was there that I felt love matched only by my family's appreciation for fresh, wholesome food, a love of good cooking, and a fellowship just not possible at a restaurant table or at the drive-in window of a fast-food outlet. These early experiences started me on my life's journey of cooking for families.

I have cooked for families in times of celebration and times of great sadness, and always these families came together to embrace the food and each other. The table is a place of communion for life's large and small events: holiday meals, weddings, birthdays, and everyday get-togethers.

We should all think about returning to the sanctity of the table, where we can rebuild our families, heal spiritually and physically, and reconnect with those we love. The table is a familiar, uncomplicated, and friendly place where we can celebrate family, friends, food, and life's many blessings.

Setting the Table

Warm, welcoming meals begin with the table.
An empty table is like a canvas, but if you take a few
minutes to consider who will be sitting at it, what
food will grace it, and what the mood of the meal is
likely to be, your instincts will guide you as to how
to set it.

The table is a familiar, uncomplicated, and friendly place where we can celebrate family, friends, food, and life's many blessings.

Seeded Cheddar Cheese Straws

Makes about 4 dozen straws

When I was working in Governor Bob Graham's kitchen in Florida, we used to bake these by the hundreds and freeze them. When the governor's staff added a reception at the last minute to the schedule, we were ready! These flaky appetizers could be the all-time perfect partner for your evening cocktail.

2 cups (8 ounces) shredded sharp
   Cheddar cheese

6 tablespoons (3/4 stick) unsalted butter, at
   room temperature

1 cup all-purpose flour

1/4 teaspoon salt

1/4 teaspoon baking powder

1/4 teaspoon freshly ground black pepper

1/8 teaspoon cayenne

1 tablespoon water

1 large egg yolk beaten with 1 teaspoon water,
   for glaze

3 teaspoons sesame seeds, poppy seeds, or black
   onion seeds (see Note), for topping

Stir the cheese and butter together in a medium bowl to combine. Sift the flour, salt, baking powder, pepper, and cayenne together. Stir into the butter with the water to make a soft dough. Divide the dough into 2 rectangles and wrap each in plastic wrap. Refrigerate until chilled, at least 1 hour and up to 8 hours. (If well chilled, let the dough stand at room temperature for 10 minutes before rolling.)

Position racks in the center and top third of the oven and preheat to 350°F.

Roll out 1 rectangle on a lightly floured work surface into a 1/4-inch-thick rectangle about 12 x 7 1/2 inches. Brush the top of the dough with some of the yolk mixture, and sprinkle with 1 1/2 teaspoons of seeds. Using a pizza wheel and a ruler, cut the dough into strips about 3/4-inch wide and 3 inches long. Place the strips 1 inch apart on ungreased baking sheets. Repeat with the remaining dough, glaze, and seeds.

Bake until crisp and lightly browned, switching the positions of the baking sheets from top to bottom and front to back halfway through baking, about 20 minutes. Cool on the baking sheets. (The straws can be prepared up to 3 days ahead and stored in airtight containers at room temperature. They can also be frozen, wrapped airtight, for up to 2 months.)

Note: *Black onion seeds (not really onion seeds but a spice properly called nigella or kalaunji) are available by mail order (see* Sources, *page 278).*

Garden Refrigerator Pickles

Makes 1 quart

Many folks make such a big deal about pickling. I rarely put up a huge batch of food that takes hours to bottle and process in a boiling-water bath (imperative for storing at room temperature). Instead, I pickle batches to refrigerate for quick consumption. These pickles are a good example. One tip – do sterilize the jar in boiling water before packing, even though you won't be water-processing afterwards.

2 cups cider vinegar

2 teaspoons plain (non-iodized) or pickling salt

1/2 teaspoon whole coriander seeds

1/2 teaspoon black peppercorns

2 Kirby cucumbers, scrubbed but not peeled and
   cut into 1/4-inch rounds or sliced into spears

1 small onion, cut into thin half-rounds

1 cup yellow or red grape tomatoes or use a
   combination of both colors

8 garlic cloves, crushed under a knife
   and peeled

1/4 cup (packed) sprigs of fresh dill

Bring the vinegar, salt, coriander, and peppercorns to a full boil in a medium saucepan over high heat. Cool completely.

Sterilize a 1-quart glass canning jar by immersing it in a pot of boiling water for 10 minutes or by running it through a full cycle of the dishwasher. The jar should be hot when adding the vegetables.

Layer the cucumbers, onion, tomatoes, garlic, and dill in the hot jar. Pour in enough of the vinegar to cover them completely. Screw on the lid. Refrigerate for at least 3 days before eating. (The pickles can be stored, covered and refrigerated, for up to 1 month.)

Farm Apple Butter

Makes 3 cups

Apple butter is worth making simply for the aroma it sends throughout the house. Not to mention what it does for muffins, toast, and even pancakes and waffles. You might want to try it on Sweet Potato-Pecan Waffles (see page 91) some morning.

3 pounds McIntosh apples, peeled, cored,
   and sliced

3 cups natural apple cider

1/4 cup honey

1/4 cup (packed) light brown sugar

1 teaspoon ground cinnamon

1/2 teaspoon ground allspice

1/8 teaspoon ground cloves

Bring the apples and cider to a boil over medium-high heat. Reduce the heat to medium-low. Simmer, uncovered, until the apples are soft, about 20 minutes.

Stir in the honey, brown sugar, cinnamon, allspice, and cloves. Cook until the apples break down for a very thick sauce, 45 minutes to 1 hour.

Cool just until warm. In batches, purée in a food processor fitted with the metal blade or a blender. If the mixture seems watery, return it to the saucepan and simmer until it thickens. (The apple butter can be prepared up to 2 months ahead, covered tightly, and refrigerated.)

Sun-Dried Tomato Pesto

Makes about 2 cups

Keep a container of this brick-red pesto in the refrigerator to toss with pasta, to stir into soups or salad dressings, or even to make a dish of scalloped potatoes into an event (see page 149).

2 cups sun-dried tomatoes packed in oil, drained

1 cup freshly grated Parmesan cheese

1/4 cup extra-virgin olive oil

1/4 cup (packed) fresh basil leaves

1/4 cup (packed) fresh parsley leaves

2 garlic cloves, crushed under a knife and peeled

Freshly ground pepper, to taste

Process all the ingredients in a food processor fitted with the metal blade until the mixture forms a coarse paste. (The pesto can be stored in an airtight container and refrigerated for up to 1 month.)

Tomato-Ginger Chutney

Makes 3 1/2 cups

This exotic chutney will liven up many dishes. Serve it with chicken burgers, pork chops, or even with grilled swordfish.

3/4 cup sugar

3/4 cup cider vinegar

1/2 teaspoon salt

4 cups ripe tomatoes, peeled, seeded, and
   chopped (see Note, page 30)

1 medium onion, finely chopped

6 garlic cloves, finely chopped

3 tablespoons peeled and finely chopped
   fresh ginger

1/2 teaspoon ground chipotle powder (see Note)

1/4 cup golden raisins

1/4 cup (2 ounces) sliced almonds, toasted

Bring the sugar, vinegar, and salt to a boil in a large nonreactive saucepan over high heat. Reduce the heat to medium and cook until reduced by half, about 10 minutes.

Stir in the tomatoes, onion, garlic, ginger, and chipotle powder. Simmer until thickened, stirring often, about 30 minutes. Stir in the raisins and almonds. Cool, cover, and refrigerate until ready to serve.

Note: *Chipotle chiles are smoked jalapeño chiles. They are sold dried, whole, and ground, or processed and packed in a spicy sauce (adobo).*

Ground chipotles are available at Latin markets and by mail order (see Sources, *page 278).*

Salsa Roja

Makes 3 cups

Here's an authentic Mexican salsa from my friend Nydia Cahue that uses tomatillos as the main ingredient. Tomatillos are actually related to gooseberries and have a husk that must be removed before serving. They're available at Latin grocers and at many large supermarkets.

1 pound tomatillos, husks removed

10 dried chiles de arbol (see Note)

One 8-ounce can tomato sauce

1/2 medium white onion, coarsely chopped

1 garlic clove, crushed

Salt

Bring a large saucepan of water to a boil over high heat. Add the tomatillos and cook just until softened, about 10 minutes. Drain.

Heat a heavy skillet (preferably cast iron) over high heat until very hot. Cook the chiles, turning frequently, until they turn a darker shade, about 3 minutes. Do not burn them. Transfer to a plate and cool. Cut open and discard the seeds and stems. (Wear plastic gloves if your hands are sensitive, and do not touch your eyes or other delicate parts of your body until you wash your hands well.)

Purée the tomatillos, chiles, tomato sauce, onion, and garlic in a blender or food processor. Season to taste with salt. Cool completely. (The salsa can be prepared up to 3 days ahead, covered, and refrigerated.)

Note: *Chiles de arbol are small dried hot chiles. They are available at Latin markets and by mail order (see* Sources, *page 278).*

Hot and Sweet Mustard

Makes 1 3/4 cups

Another everyday condiment that can be made quickly. This great sandwich spread was first served to me by Annella Schomburger of Tallahassee, Florida. She made me a wonderful baked ham sandwich one day when she thought I needed nourishment. Well, I have never forgotten this mustard and will never forget Annella's love for me.

1 cup dry mustard powder, preferably Coleman's

1 cup apple cider vinegar

4 large egg yolks

1 cup (packed) light brown sugar

Whisk the mustard powder and vinegar together in a bowl. Cover and refrigerate overnight.

Whisk the egg yolks and brown sugar into the mustard mixture. Place in a double boiler and insert over a saucepan of simmering water. Cook over medium heat, stirring constantly with a rubber spatula and scraping down the sides, until the mustard is thickened (an instant-read thermometer will read 160°F), about 5 minutes. Remove from the heat and cool completely. (The mustard can be stored, covered and refrigerated, for up to 1 month.)

Homemade Ketchup

Makes about 4 cups

What's nice about homemade ketchup is that you can fool around with the spices and sugar to get the flavor you like. This one is on the sweet and spicy side. If you don't like the strong taste of pickling spices, remove them halfway through the cooking period.

2 tablespoons pickling spices

10 large ripe tomatoes (about 5 pounds), peeled and coarsely chopped (see Note)

2 large onions, peeled and thinly sliced

2 celery ribs with leaves, chopped

1 cup distilled white vinegar

1/4 teaspoon ground cloves

1/4 teaspoon ground ginger

3/4 cup (packed) light brown sugar

Salt

Wrap the pickling spices in a square of rinsed cheesecloth. Place the tomatoes in a large pot along with the pickling spices, onions, celery, vinegar, cloves, and ginger. Bring to a boil and cook for 1 hour.

Add the brown sugar and cook for 2 1/2 hours, stirring often, until the ketchup thickens. Season to taste with salt.

Remove the bag of pickling spices. Purée the ketchup in a food processor fitted with the metal blade. Strain through a wire sieve to remove the seeds. Return the strained purée to the pot and cook for 15 to 20 minutes. Pour into a container and refrigerate.

Note: *To peel tomatoes, bring a large pot of water to a boil over high heat. Add the tomatoes and cook until the skins loosen, about 1 minute. As each tomato is ready, lift it out of the water with a slotted spoon and place in a bowl of water. Core, peel, and coarsely chop the tomatoes.*

Spiced Maple Pecans

Makes 4 cups

While these are irresistible any time of the year, you'll find it wise to make a batch at the beginning of the holiday entertaining season to have ready for drop-in visitors.

1 pound pecan halves (about 4 cups)

1/4 cup light corn syrup

1/4 cup pure maple syrup

3 tablespoons sugar

2 teaspoons ground cumin

2 teaspoons sweet paprika

2 teaspoons chile powder

1 teaspoon salt

1/8 teaspoon cayenne

Position a rack in the center of the oven and preheat to 350°F.

Spread the pecans in a large roasting pan and bake until lightly toasted, about 8 minutes.

Combine the corn and maple syrups. Pour over the nuts and toss to coat well. Bake, stirring occasionally, until the nuts have absorbed most of the syrup, about 10 minutes.

Mix the sugar, cumin, paprika, chile powder, salt, and cayenne. Pour the nuts into a bowl. Toss with a spoon, gradually adding the sugar mixture, until the nuts are coated with the sugar. Cool slightly and break apart any nuts that are sticking together. Pour onto a baking sheet and cool completely. (The nuts can be stored in an airtight container at room temperature for up to 1 week.)

Homemade Mayonnaise

Makes about 1 1/2 cups

I think you'll be surprised at how easy it is to make your own mayonnaise – and it tastes fantastic. Because it is made with raw eggs, never allow a recipe that contains it to stand out for more than two hours at room temperature.

1 large egg, at room temperature (see Note)

2 tablespoons fresh lemon juice

2 teaspoons Dijon mustard

3/4 cup canola oil

3/4 cup olive oil (not extra-virgin)

1/4 teaspoon salt

1/8 teaspoon freshly ground pepper

Put the egg, lemon juice, and mustard in a food processor and pulse to blend.

Combine the canola and olive oils in a glass measuring cup. With the machine running, add the oil in a slow steady stream until the mayonnaise thickens. Season with salt and pepper. (The mayonnaise can be prepared up to 3 days ahead, covered, and refrigerated.)

Note: *This recipe uses a raw egg. Eggs have been known to carry the harmful salmonella bacteria. To reduce the risk of infection, use only fresh, clean, refrigerated eggs that are free of any cracks.*

If a recipe calls for room temperature eggs, place the uncracked eggs in a bowl of hot water for 5 minutes so they can lose their chill.

Do not serve raw eggs to very young or elderly people or to anyone with a weakened immune system.

Ice Box Buttermilk Dressing

Makes about 2 cups

Fans of thick and creamy salad dressing will love this. I like to make it in a glass jar to store in the refrigerator – just give it a good shake to mix everything up before serving.

1/2 cup extra-virgin olive oil

1/2 cup reduced-fat mayonnaise

1/2 cup buttermilk

2 tablespoons grainy mustard, such as moutarde de Meaux

2 tablespoons red wine vinegar

2 tablespoons chopped rinsed capers

2 tablespoons minced shallots

2 teaspoons chopped fresh oregano

1 teaspoon chopped fresh basil

1 teaspoon chopped fresh tarragon

1 teaspoon sugar

Salt and hot red pepper sauce, to taste

Place all the ingredients in a jar and shake well to blend. (The dressing can be prepared up to 1 week ahead, covered, and refrigerated.)

ice box
dressing

Roasted Tomato Sauce

Makes 3 cups

I used to make my tomato sauce like everyone else, simmering fresh tomatoes in a big pot until I discovered the big, intense tomato flavor of sauce made with roasted tomatoes.

5 tablespoons extra-virgin olive oil

3 pounds Roma or plum tomatoes, cut lengthwise in halves

Salt and freshly ground pepper

2 garlic cloves, minced

1/4 teaspoon crushed red pepper

1/4 cup fresh basil leaves, cut into thin ribbons

Position a rack in the center of the oven and preheat to 450°F. Generously brush a large baking sheet with 1 tablespoon of the olive oil.

Season the cut sides of the tomatoes with salt and pepper. Place, cut side down, on the baking sheet. Brush the skins with 2 tablespoons of the olive oil. Bake until the tomato skins are lightly browned and the tomatoes are tender, 30 to 35 minutes. Cool completely. Pull the skins off the tomatoes and discard.

Meanwhile, heat the remaining 2 tablespoons of olive oil, the garlic, and red pepper in a small skillet over medium heat until the garlic has softened but has not browned, about 2 minutes. Purée the tomatoes and garlic oil in a food processor fitted with the metal blade. Stir in the basil and season to taste with salt and pepper. Serve hot. (The sauce can be prepared up to 3 days ahead, cooled, covered, and refrigerated, or frozen for up to 2 months.)

Oven-Roasted Tomatoes

Makes 2 cups

Roasting tomatoes at a high temperature brings out their natural sweetness. Preparing tomatoes this way is especially good when you use farm-stand tomatoes, but it does wonders with the ones from the supermarket, which aren't as tasty.

1/4 cup extra-virgin olive oil, as needed

2 pounds ripe Roma or plum tomatoes

Salt and freshly ground black pepper

1 tablespoon chopped fresh thyme, marjoram,
   or oregano

Position a rack in the center of the oven and preheat to 450°F. Generously brush a large baking sheet with some of the oil.

Cut the tomatoes in half lengthwise. Season the cut sides with salt, pepper, and chopped herbs. Place, cut side down, on the baking sheet. Brush the skins with oil.

Bake until the tomato skins are lightly browned and the tomatoes are tender, 30 to 35 minutes.

Cool completely. Pull the skins off the tomatoes. Use immediately, or store in a covered container, covered with additional olive oil. (The tomatoes can be stored, covered with oil, and refrigerated, for up to 1 week. To remove from the oil, let stand at room temperature until the oil melts.)

Walnut and Late Harvest Riesling Vinaigrette

Makes 1 1/2 cups

This slightly sweet salad dressing allows me to indulge in two of my favorite ingredients, walnut mustard and late harvest Riesling vinegar. Even with Dijon mustard and any fruit-flavored vinegar, you will get a great vinaigrette.

1 tablespoon of mayonnaise

2 tablespoons Laurent de Clos Walnut Mustard
(see Note) or Dijon mustard

1 garlic clove

1/4 cup Cuisine Perel Late Harvest Riesling
Vinegar (see Note)

1 cup extra-virgin olive oil

Salt and freshly ground pepper

Put the mayonnaise, mustard and garlic in a blender and process until smooth. Add the vinegar and process to combine. With the blender running, slowly add the olive oil in a steady stream until the dressing thickens. Season to taste with salt and pepper. (The dressing can be prepared up to 3 days ahead, covered, and refrigerated.)

Note: *Laurent de Clos Walnut Mustard and Cuisine Perel Late Harvest Riesling Vinegar are available at specialty food stores and by mail order (see* Sources, *page 278).*

Red Pepper Vinegar

Makes about 2 cups

This simple sauce, which can be made in no time and keeps forever, is found on every Southern table. It adds a picante flavor to all types of food.

2 cups white wine vinegar, preferably
champagne vinegar

4 garlic cloves, peeled

2 teaspoons salt

8 whole black peppercorns

1 cup whole fresh serrano chiles

Combine the vinegar, garlic, salt, and peppercorns in a medium saucepan. Bring to a boil over medium-high heat. Remove from the heat.

Place the chiles in a glass or other nonreactive container. Pour the hot vinegar mixture over the chiles, cover, and allow to steep for 2 weeks before using. (The vinegar can be stored for up to 6 months in a cool, dark place.)

East Hampton Strawberry Jam

Makes 3 half-pints

When I was cooking in East Hampton, I loved buying strawberries from the many small farms on the South Fork and turning them into jam. The farmers taught me that dry weather meant flavorful berries, so I would keep my fingers crossed for sunny weather more for good jam berries than for getting a suntan. Even today, it just isn't summer until I make this jam for my morning toast or waffles.

5 cups hulled and halved strawberries

  (about 2^1/2 pints)

4 cups sugar

1^1/2 cups water

1 tablespoon fresh lemon juice

The night before making the jam, toss the berries with 1 cup of the sugar. Cover and refrigerate overnight.

Drain the berries, reserving the juice. Bring the remaining 3 cups of sugar, the water, strawberry juice, and lemon juice to a full boil in a 5-quart pot over medium heat, stirring to dissolve the sugar. Add the berries. Reduce the heat to medium and cook, stirring occasionally, until the syrup is thick and a candy thermometer reads 238°F, about 30 minutes. Without a candy thermometer, pour a spoonful of the syrup on a chilled plate. If it forms a pool without running, the jam is set.

Meanwhile, boil 3 half-pint canning jars in boiling water for 10 minutes. Soak the rings and lids in a bowl of hot water. Drain the jars, rings, and lids. Place the jars on a folded towel or wood surface.

Ladle the hot jam into the hot jars, leaving ^{1}/2-inch of head space. Attach the lids and screw on the rings. Let stand until completely cooled. (The jam will keep indefinitely in a cool dark place. Refrigerate after opening.)

Beverages for the Table

Holiday Hot Chocolate

Makes 2 servings

Cocoa powder has so much flavor and can be mixed with skim milk to make a very satisfying hot drink. For an extra treat, make foam from additional cold skim milk in a milk frother according to the manufacturer's instructions and spoon the froth on top.

^{1}/4 cup unsweetened cocoa powder

2^1/2 tablespoons sugar or artificial

  sweetener to taste

2 cups skim milk

Chocolate shavings, for garnish (optional)

Whisk together cocoa powder and sugar in a microwave-safe cup. Microwave the milk on high until very hot, about 1 minute. Whisk about ^{1}/4 cup of the hot milk into the cocoa mixture to make a paste, then whisk in the remaining milk until smooth. Garnish with chocolate shavings, if using. Serve immediately.

Where I come from, iced tea is sometimes called "the wine of the South," and it's always sweetened. They say the closer you live to a cane field, the sweeter the tea.

Tropical Fruit Sun Tea

Makes 8 to 10 servings

For crystal-clear iced tea, never use boiling water. That is one of the reasons iced tea that has been gently steeped in bright sunlight is so popular. While you're steeping the tea, why not add more flavors by tossing in some orange and lemon zest? For the strongest fruit flavor, use fruit-flavored black tea. You can use herbal fruit teas, but increase the amount of tea by about half. Use either loose tea or tea bags.

1 cup loose fruit-flavored tea or 12 tea bags

Zest of $1/2$ lemon

Zest of $1/2$ orange

1 cinnamon stick

$1/4$ cup sliced crystallized ginger

10 cups water, preferably bottled spring water

Orange slices, for garnish

Place the tea leaves, lemon and orange zests, cinnamon stick, and ginger on a large square of rinsed cheesecloth. Tie into a bundle to create a bag.

Pour water into a clear glass jar. Add the bag or tea bags and place the jar in a sunny place. Steep until the tea is full flavored, 2 to 3 hours. Remove the bags and refrigerate until ready to serve.

Serve in ice-filled glasses and garnish with the orange slices.

Vanilla Citrus Punch

Makes 4 to 6 servings

This great punch was created by my friend Karen Armijo for a Fourth of July celebration in East Hampton. The punch is perfect for the whole family but can be made wicked for adults by adding your favorite dark rum.

3 cups fresh orange juice

1 cup fresh or unsweetened canned
   pineapple juice

$1/4$ cup fresh lime juice

$1/4$ cup fresh lemon juice

1 whole vanilla bean

$1 1/2$ cups ginger ale or club soda, chilled

Combine all the juices in a large pitcher. Split the vanilla bean lengthwise and scrape the seeds into the juice. Stir with a whisk to separate the vanilla seeds. Cover and refrigerate until chilled, at least 2 hours or overnight.

Just before serving, add the ginger ale. Serve in ice-filled glasses.

Sparkling Lemonade

Makes 4 to 6 servings

Sparkling water makes lemonade even more refreshing. This version is on the tart side. You can certainly make it sweeter, or even substitute artificial sweetener for the sugar, if you prefer.

8 large lemons

3/4 cup sugar

6 cups cold, sparkling water

Lemon slices and fresh mint leaves, for garnish

Wash and squeeze the juice from the lemons, reserving the lemon skins. Strain the juice into a pitcher. Add the lemon skins and sugar. Using a wooden spoon, crush the lemon skins into the juice and sugar to release the oils.

Add the sparkling water and stir to mix well. Refrigerate until ready to serve.

Serve in ice-filled glasses and garnish with lemon slices and fresh mint leaves.

Mulled Apple Cider

Makes 4 servings

Every fall this is my most requested beverage for those cold windy days and nights in the Midwest. To make it really special, look for organic natural apple cider at your local health food store and create your own tussy-mussy of spices.

1 large navel orange

1 lemon

Three 3-inch cinnamon sticks

1 tablespoon allspice berries

1 teaspoon whole cloves

2 tablespoons chopped crystallized ginger

1 quart pure apple cider

1/4 cup (packed) light brown sugar

Orange slices, for garnish

Using a vegetable peeler, remove the zest from the orange and lemon, then squeeze the juice and reserve. Wrap the lemon and orange zest, cinnamon, allspice, cloves, and ginger in a piece of rinsed cheesecloth and tie into a packet.

Combine the apple cider, orange and lemon juice, brown sugar, and spice packet in a medium nonreactive saucepan. Bring to a simmer over medium heat. Reduce the heat to low and simmer for 5 minutes.

Ladle into cups and garnish with the orange slices. Serve hot.

Mango Kiwi Smoothie

Serves 1

Time is of the essence in the morning. The night before, place the cut-up fruit in the freezer so it is frozen in the morning when you're ready to toss it into the blender. Of course you can add a spoonful of yogurt to the smoothie if you have some in the refrigerator. Ground flax seed or wheat germ add extra vitamins and roughage.

1¼ cups sparkling water, unfiltered apple juice,
    or low-fat milk, as needed

1 ripe mango, peeled, pitted, and cut into
    pieces, frozen

1 kiwi, peeled and cut into pieces, frozen

2 tablespoons honey

Combine the sparkling water, mango, kiwi, and honey in a blender. Purée until smooth. Add additional sparkling water as needed to achieve the consistency you prefer. Serve immediately.

Vegetable Broth

Makes about 3 1/2 quarts

Here is a light, simple broth for your vegetable soups. If you prefer a stronger broth, make a double batch and boil the strained broth over high heat until reduced by half. You can leave out the chard if you don't have it, but consider buying a bunch for the broth. Don't salt this broth – it will have more versatility if you season the finished dish instead.

8 cups water, preferably bottled spring water

1 large onion, chopped

1 large leek, white part only, chopped
    and rinsed

2 medium carrots, chopped

3 celery ribs, chopped

1 cup sliced mushrooms

1 cup chopped Swiss chard leaves (optional)

2 sprigs of fresh thyme or 1/4 teaspoon
    dried thyme

4 sprigs of fresh parsley

1/4 teaspoon whole black peppercorns

1 bay leaf

Combine all the ingredients in a large soup pot. Bring to a boil over high heat. Reduce the heat to medium-low and simmer until well flavored, about 1 hour.

Strain the broth, discarding the solids, and cool to room temperature. Cover and refrigerate (The broth can be prepared up to 3 days ahead, covered, and refrigerated, or frozen for up to 3 months.)

Chicken Broth

Makes about 3 quarts

I use chicken broth in a lot of recipes, so I like to have a surplus supply in the freezer ready to put into action.

3 1/2 pounds chicken wings, chopped at
    the joints

1 medium onion, chopped

1 medium carrot, chopped

1 celery rib, chopped

1 tablespoon vegetable oil

4 sprigs of fresh parsley

3 sprigs of fresh thyme or 1/2 teaspoon
    dried thyme

1/2 teaspoon whole black peppercorns

2 bay leaves

Cook the chicken wings, onion, carrot, and celery in the oil in a large pot over medium-high heat, stirring often, just until the vegetables soften (the chicken should not brown), about 10 minutes.

Add enough cold water to the pot to cover the ingredients by 2 inches. Bring to a boil over high heat, skimming off any foam that rises to the surface. Add the parsley, thyme, peppercorns, and bay leaves. Reduce the heat to low and simmer, uncovered, until the broth is full-flavored, at least 2 hours and up to 6 hours.

Strain the broth through a colander set over a large bowl. Discard the solids. Let stand for 5 minutes. Skim off the clear yellow fat that rises to the surface. Cool to room temperature. Cover and refrigerate until ready to use. (The broth can be prepared up to 3 days ahead, covered, and refrigerated, or frozen for up to 3 months.)

Beef Broth

Makes about 1 1/2 quarts

There is a lot of canned beef broth on supermarket shelves, but nothing beats the flavor of homemade broth. The best is made from a combination of bones and meaty but bony cuts like oxtails and with total disregard for rushing the simmering.

3 to 4 pounds beef bones or a combination
    of bones, oxtails, or short ribs

Water, as needed

1 large onion, coarsely chopped

2 medium leeks, white parts only,
    coarsely chopped and rinsed

2 medium carrots, coarsely chopped

1 celery rib, with leaves,
    coarsely chopped

1 1/2 teaspoons tomato paste (optional)

4 sprigs of fresh thyme or 1/2 teaspoon
    dried thyme

4 sprigs of fresh parsley

1/4 teaspoon whole black peppercorns

1 bay leaf

Position a rack in the top third of the oven and preheat to 450°F.

Spread the bones in a roasting pan. Bake until the bones are browned, about 30 minutes.

Transfer the bones to a stockpot. Pour the fat out of the pan. Place the roasting pan over high heat on top of the stove. Pour 2 cups water into the pan, scraping up the browned bits in the pan with a wooden spoon. Pour this liquid into the stockpot. Add the onion, leeks, carrots, and celery. Add enough water to cover the bones by 2 inches.

Bring to a boil over high heat, skimming off the foam that rises to the surface. Add the tomato paste (if using), thyme, parsley, peppercorns, and bay leaf. Reduce the heat to low. Simmer, uncovered, until the broth is full flavored, at least 2 hours and up to 8 hours, the longer the better.

Strain the broth through a colander into a large bowl. Discard the solids. Let stand for 10 minutes. Skim off the clear yellow fat on the surface. Cool the broth to room temperature. Cover tightly and refrigerate. (The broth can be prepared up to 3 days ahead, covered, and refrigerated, or frozen for up to 3 months.)

Bless the Table

Daily we must unite with the human family around the world by counting our blessings over the table. These opening remarks start the celebration of the meal and of life, and express our love.

Blessing

Two footed, four footed, or from the earth cajoled
This meal, a miracle of sacrifice, is a call for reverence.
A meal of wonder, our eyes do behold
Let us give thanks for its sustenance.

Eric Copage
Author of Black Pearls

We are grateful to be together with open hearts.
We are grateful for the miracle of food.
We are grateful for the miracle of each other.
Food is holy. We are holy. Bless this food. Bless us.
Thank you, thank you,
thank you.

Gary Zukav
Author of The Seat of the Soul

Blessing

Let us give thanks for nature's abundance at this table
this evening and for the work of loving hands.

Thank you, Sacred Spirit, for your presence
in this moment and in this meal.
We feel your love joining us heart to heart
as we pause to appreciate this special time together.
We recognize your power in the nourishment
this food represents and in the joy with
which it is prepared and shared.
We extend the love and nourishment of this meal
and this moment to all beings everywhere,
dissolving every sense of fear or lack.
Thank you, Sacred Spirit, for your constant
presence as light, love, and laughter,
within and around us, on the great spiritual
journey we share with all of life.

Amen!

Reverend Ed Townley
Senior Minister, Unity in Chicago

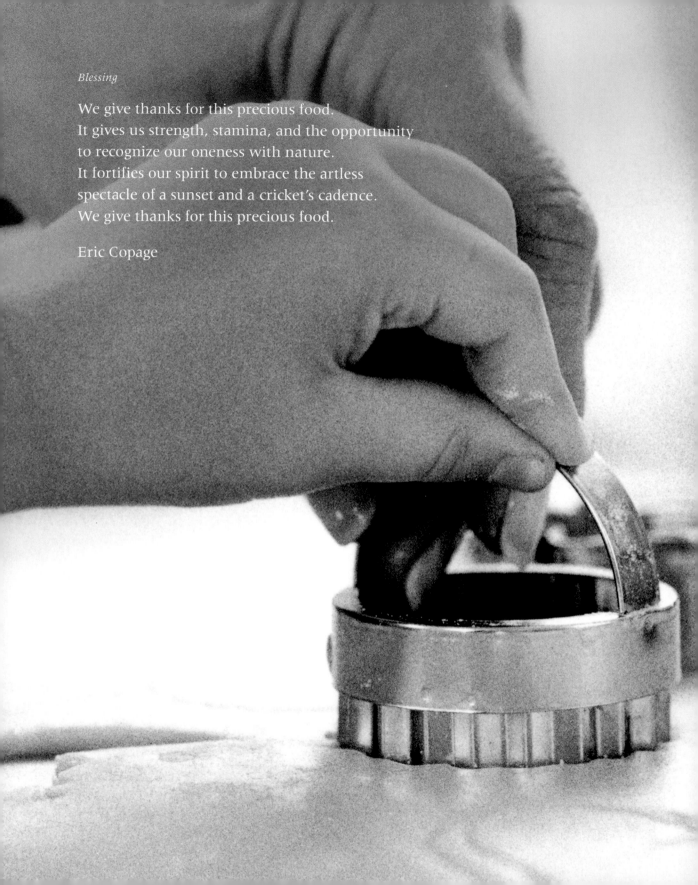

Blessing

We give thanks for this precious food.
It gives us strength, stamina, and the opportunity
to recognize our oneness with nature.
It fortifies our spirit to embrace the artless
spectacle of a sunset and a cricket's cadence.
We give thanks for this precious food.

Eric Copage

Breaking Bread

Universally, bread is a symbol for sharing. As it passes from one to the other around the table, bread nourishes and comforts as few other foods do.

Since ancient times, bread has been symbolic of plenty. It stands out as the meal's most sacred course. A Southern meal is just not complete without it. All my life, bread has been part of every meal.

I remember baskets of steaming breads wrapped in checkered cloth napkins being passed around the table as soon as we sat down. We'd often sneak an extra roll or slice of bread when we thought no one was looking. If hot biscuits made with bacon drippings and soft white flour were the order of the day, I could barely wait while my grandfather, a deacon at the First Baptist Church, said the blessing. But I know now how significant the ritual blessing of bread was to our family.

The bread was served with fresh creamy butter, the likes of which is hard to find today. If we were visiting my mother's family, someone would have recently milked old Jersey and filled a jar with her rich milk. Before dinner, we gathered on the porch with Aunt Viola and Uncle Wilbert and took turns shaking the jar until the cream turned into butter. What sheer delight it was tasting the freshness of that butter. I once told my mother it tasted "like grass," and she laughed when she explained that grass was what Jersey ate. Smearing copious amounts of it on warm Fluffy Yeast Biscuits or Classic Southern Cornbread is indeed a fond memory. We used any leftover cream to make the lightest, most tender biscuits you ever tasted!

I still serve bread with every meal, ignoring anyone's concerns about excessive carbohydrates. Who can forsake bread? To give it up entirely would be, for me, like giving up sleep. I could not function in life without it. Nor could I imagine not being able to share this symbolic food with my friends and my family.

Recently I was asked to participate in the Chicago fund-raiser for Share Our Strength, a national organization committed to fighting hunger. I was thrilled to be part of this worthwhile cause and suggested I turn out dozens of my famous Fluffy Yeast Biscuits (which down South are sometimes called angel biscuits) to serve with the oyster stew. I found myself focusing on the biscuits—I so wanted them to be perfectly light and tender—and relying heavily on my assistant chef, Karen Armijo, to tend to the stew. Making biscuits, which I had done so many times before—sifting the flour and gently cutting the butter into it—became my evening's meditation. It was an art that reminded me of who I was. Such meditation in the harried environment of a restaurant kitchen reminded me of why I, as a cook, chose to devote my professional life to cooking for families.

While cooking for families, I was constantly reminded that we are all human, capable of making mistakes, of hurting those we love, and, most of all, capable of forgiveness. I see this over and over again at the table.

The act of cooking for others, making dishes they especially like and sharing your own favorites, is an act of love. It says to those we cook for that we revere and bless them for being part of our lives.

I want to share both the wonderful breads of my heritage and others I came to appreciate later in life. I've never forgotten my grandmother's Boarding House Biscuits, which she made in a handsome hand-hewn wooden bowl shaped so that the flour could sit at one end and be pulled into the dough as it was kneaded. After it was patted and rolled, the dough was cut and the biscuits baked on a well-worn, darkened pan, then taken piping hot from the oven. Can't you imagine how wonderful that moment was!

The aroma of baking bread is irresistible. All home-baked breads elicit smiles when they appear on the table, and since bread is really so easy to make, it's worth the small effort. It's been my experience that even a mediocre meal is saved by great bread!

Fluffy Yeast Biscuits

Makes about 2 dozen biscuits

For those of you who like light and fluffy biscuits instead of the "crisp on the outside and tender within" variety, here's a recipe that uses yeast to ensure that they rise to the desired heights. You can refrigerate the dough overnight so you can have a big plate of biscuits ready for breakfast in no time.

Two $1/4$-ounce packages active dry yeast

$1/4$ cup warm (105° to 115°F) water

4 cups self-rising flour (see Note)

2 tablespoons sugar

1 teaspoon baking soda

4 tablespoons ($1/2$ stick) unsalted butter, chilled, cut into thin slices

$1/4$ cup vegetable shortening, chilled, cut up

$1^{1}/2$ cups buttermilk, as needed

Sprinkle the yeast over the warm water in a small bowl and let stand for 5 minutes. Stir to dissolve the yeast.

Sift the flour, sugar, and baking soda in a large bowl. Add the butter and shortening. Using a pastry blender or 2 knives, cut the butter and shortening into the flour until the mixture looks crumbly with a few pea-size pieces of fat.

Make a well in the center, and add the yeast mixture. Stir in enough of the buttermilk to make a moist, shaggy dough. Knead in the bowl a few times, just until the dough comes together.

Transfer the dough to a medium bowl (no need to oil the bowl). Cover tightly with plastic wrap. Let stand at room temperature until the dough doubles in volume, about 45 minutes. (The dough can be made up to 1 day ahead, covered tightly with plastic wrap, and refrigerated.)

Position racks in the center and top third of the oven and preheat to 400°F.

Pat down the dough. Transfer to a lightly floured work surface. Pat or roll out the dough until $1/2$-inch thick. Using a $2^{1}/2$-inch biscuit cutter, cut out the biscuits and place them 1 inch apart on ungreased baking sheets. Gather up the scraps, knead together, and roll and cut out more biscuits until all of the dough is used.

Bake, switching the positions of the sheets from top to bottom and front to back halfway through baking, until the biscuits are golden brown, about 20 minutes. Serve hot.

Note: *I use self-rising flour (which contains baking powder and salt) in many of my recipes. Because I often seem to be cooking in a hurry, I like the convenience of not having to measure one more ingredient.*

Also, I'll admit that my Southern relatives use it as a matter of course. I learned so much about cooking from them, I never bothered to change some of my favorite recipes over to all-purpose flour and baking powder. I'll bet that you'll like the convenience of self-rising flour, too.

Golden Challah

Makes 2 large loaves

I am fascinated by the many different breads in Jewish culture, from the austere, unleavened matzo to the egg-rich braided challah. This recipe comes from my friend Paula Golden, so when I think of this bread, I not only think of the bread's color but of the person who gave me the recipe as well.

2¹/₂ cups warm (105°F to 115°F) water

Two ¹/₄-ounce packages active dry yeast

9 cups unbleached flour, as needed

³/₄ cup sugar

³/₄ cup vegetable oil, such as canola

3 large eggs, beaten

1 tablespoon salt

1 teaspoon vanilla extract

¹/₂ teaspoon baking powder

¹/₂ teaspoon ground cinnamon

1 large egg, beaten, for glaze

Mix 1 cup of the warm water and the yeast in the bowl of a heavy-duty mixer and let stand for 5 minutes. Stir to dissolve the yeast. Stir in 1 cup of the flour to make a thick batter. Sprinkle another 1 cup of flour on top of the batter. Let stand in a warm place, uncovered, until the batter begins to bubble up through the flour crust, about 30 minutes.

Add the sugar, oil, eggs, salt, vanilla, baking powder, and cinnamon and mix well. Attach the bowl to the mixer and fit with the paddle blade. On low speed, gradually add enough of the flour to make a stiff dough that cleans the sides of the bowl. Change to the dough hook, and knead until smooth and supple, about 10 minutes. Transfer to a lightly floured work surface and shape into a ball.

Lightly oil a large bowl. Place the dough in the bowl and turn to coat with oil. Cover the bowl tightly with plastic wrap. Let stand in a warm place until almost doubled in volume, about 45 minutes. Knead by hand on an unfloured work surface for 5 minutes. Return to the bowl, turn to coat, cover, and let stand until doubled in volume, about 45 minutes.

Divide the dough in half. Cut each portion of dough into thirds, and shape each into a thick log. Keeping the other logs of dough covered with plastic wrap, shape each log into a rope about 20 inches long. (This is easiest to do by rolling the log under your hands, pressing down on it with your palms, and moving your hands apart as you roll to stretch into a rope.) If the dough resists, cover with plastic wrap and set aside for 5 minutes, then try again.

Lightly oil 2 large baking sheets. Line up 3 ropes next to each other and perpendicular to yourself. Braid the ropes, starting at the center and working to one end. Pinch the ends of the braid together. Flip the dough over with the unbraided ropes facing you. Braid from the center to the other end, and pinch the ends together. Transfer the loaf to a baking sheet. Repeat with the other 3 ropes of dough.

Cover each loaf with plastic wrap and let stand in a warm place until puffed and doubled in volume, about 40 minutes.

Meanwhile, position racks in the bottom and top thirds of the oven and preheat to 350°F.

Brush each loaf with some of the beaten egg. Bake, switching the positions of the sheets from top to bottom and front to back halfway through baking, until the loaves are golden brown and sound hollow when tapped on the bottom, about 45 minutes. If you wish, brush the loaves with additional glaze to cover any new surfaces that rise during baking – you want an evenly glazed loaf. Cool completely.

Cheddar Batter Bread

Makes 2 loaves

No kneading needed with this moist, flavorful bread. This recipe makes two loaves, so you'll probably want to freeze one. Toast a slice and slather it with Farm Apple Butter (see page 27) for a real treat.

4 tablespoons (^{1}/2 stick) unsalted butter

^{3}/4 cup buttermilk

^{3}/4 cup water

One ^{1}/4-ounce package active dry yeast

3 large eggs

1 teaspoon hot red pepper sauce

4 cups all-purpose flour

2 tablespoons sugar

1 tablespoon baking powder

1 teaspoon baking soda

1 teaspoon salt

^{1}/4 cup freshly grated Parmesan cheese

1 cup (4 ounces) shredded sharp Cheddar or Swiss cheese

1 large egg yolk beaten with 1 tablespoon water, for glaze

Heat the butter in a medium saucepan over medium heat. Add the buttermilk and water and heat just until warm to the touch (105° to 115°F). Pour into a large bowl. Sprinkle the yeast on top and let stand for 5 minutes. Whisk to dissolve the yeast. Whisk in the eggs and hot sauce.

Sift together flour, sugar, baking powder, baking soda, and salt. Gradually stir into the liquid to make a thick batter. Stir in the Parmesan cheese and ^{3}/4 cup of the Cheddar cheese.

Lightly butter two 8^1/2 x 4^1/2 x 2^1/2-inch loaf pans. Spread the batter evenly in the pans. Cover loosely with plastic wrap and let stand in a warm place until doubled in volume, about 45 minutes.

Position a rack in the center of the oven and preheat to 375°F.

Brush the tops of the loaves with the egg mixture. Bake 25 minutes. Sprinkle the tops of the loaves with the remaining ^{1}/4 cup of shredded Cheddar and bake until the loaves are golden and sound hollow when removed from the pans and tapped on the bottoms, 10 to 15 minutes.

Cool in pans for 10 minutes. Turn out onto wire racks and cool completely. (The breads can be made 2 days ahead, wrapped in aluminum foil, and stored at room temperature.)

Naan continued

If it is too dry, add a tablespoon of water and process. Knead the ball of dough in the machine for 45 seconds.

Empty the dough onto a lightly floured surface, knead briefly, and form into a ball. Lightly oil the inside of a large bowl. Place the ball of dough in the bowl and turn to coat with the oil. Cover the bowl tightly with plastic wrap. Let stand in a warm place until doubled in volume, about 1 hour.

Punch down the dough and knead on a clean surface for 2 minutes. Divide the dough into 6 equal pieces, form into balls, and cover loosely with plastic wrap. Working 1 ball at a time and keeping the others covered, roll and pull each piece of dough into a tear shape about 10 inches long and 5 inches wide. If the dough retracts, set aside, covered with plastic wrap, and let rest for 5 minutes before trying again. Lightly brush the tops with oil and sprinkle with sesame seeds (if using). Cover the breads loosely with plastic wrap.

Using a well-floured baker's peel or an unrimmed cookie sheet, slide 2 or 3 breads onto the baking stone. Bake until puffed and golden, 6 to 8 minutes. Repeat with the remaining dough. Serve warm.

Grilled Parmesan Flatbread

Makes 4 to 6 servings

In the summer of 1999, we had a big street party, and I created this bread for the grill. It was a hit of the party!

Pizza Dough (page 188)

3 tablespoons extra-virgin olive oil

1/2 cup (2 ounces) freshly grated
  Parmesan cheese

Build a charcoal fire in an outdoor grill and let it burn until the coals are medium-hot (you should be able to hold your hand just above the grate for 3 seconds). On a gas grill, preheat on High, then turn to Medium.

Roll out the dough on an unfloured work surface until about 1/4-inch thick. It doesn't have to be round – make any irregular shape. Transfer the dough to a very lightly floured rimless baking sheet.

Lightly oil the grill grate. Slide the dough off the sheet onto the grate. Brush the top of the dough with some of the oil. Cover and grill until the underside of the dough is set, 3 to 4 minutes. (If the dough begins to scorch, the coals are too hot. Move the dough to a cooler area, near but not directly over the coals. For a gas grill, turn to Low.) Turn the flatbread, brush off any flour, and brush with the remaining oil. Sprinkle with the cheese. Cover and grill until the other side is firm and the cheese is melted, about 4 minutes more.

Use the baking sheet to transfer the flatbread to a serving platter. Cool briefly, then serve warm, allowing the guests to tear the bread into servings.

Focaccia with Roasted Tomatoes and Onion

Makes 8 to 12 servings

For an Italian menu, serve this thick flatbread that has been embellished with roasted tomatoes and caramelized shreds of onion. When sautéing the onion, don't take it past the translucent stage, as it will continue to cook in the oven and eventually caramelize to golden brown.

Dough

1 cup warm (105° to 115°F) water

1/2 teaspoon sugar

One 1/4-ounce package active dry yeast

1/4 cup extra-virgin olive oil

1 1/2 teaspoons salt

3 cups unbleached flour, as needed

1/4 cup chopped fresh basil

Topping

2 tablespoons extra-virgin olive oil

3 medium onions, cut into 1/4-inch-thick
half-moons

Salt and freshly ground black pepper

2 cups Oven-Roasted Tomatoes (page 34)

1/2 cup freshly grated Parmesan cheese

To make the dough, pour 1/4 cup of the water into the bowl of a heavy-duty mixer and add the sugar. Sprinkle the yeast on top. Let stand until the yeast softens, about 5 minutes. Stir to dissolve.

Stir in the remaining 3/4 cup of water, the oil, and salt. Attach the paddle blade and mix on low speed. Gradually add enough of the flour to make a soft dough. Change to the dough hook and increase the speed to medium. Knead until the dough is smooth and supple, about 10 minutes. During the last few minutes, add the basil.

Lightly oil a large bowl. Turn the dough out onto a clean work surface, knead briefly, and shape into a ball. Place the dough in the bowl and turn to coat on all sides. Cover tightly with plastic wrap. Let stand in a warm place until doubled in volume, about 1 hour.

To make the topping, heat the oil in a large skillet over medium heat. Add the onions and cook, stirring occasionally, until they turn golden, about 10 minutes. Season lightly with salt and pepper and cool.

Lightly oil a 17 x 11-inch jelly-roll pan. Punch down the dough and place in the pan. Pat and pull the dough to spread it evenly in the pan. (If the dough pulls back, cover loosely with plastic wrap, let stand for 5 minutes, then try again.) Cover loosely with plastic wrap and let stand in a warm place until puffy, about 30 minutes.

Position a rack in the lower third of the oven, place a baking stone on the rack, and preheat the oven to 425°F.

Arrange the tomatoes over the top of the dough, then the onions. Sprinkle with the cheese and grind pepper over all. Bake until the focaccia is golden brown, about 30 minutes. Cool slightly, then cut into pieces to serve.

Note: *You can purchase a baking stone from www.bridgekitchenware.com.*

Classic Southern Cornbread

Makes 8 servings

To make good cornbread, you must have good cornmeal. What do I mean by that? It should have a coarse, sandy texture – most of the cornmeal from big companies is just too fine. Stoneground cornmeal, available at natural food stores and many supermarkets, is best. Be sure the cornmeal is fresh, as it contains oils that can turn rancid easily. As a precaution, always store your cornmeal in the refrigerator (something Southern cooks rarely have to do because they use up the cornmeal so quickly it doesn't have a chance to turn on them). Use a well-seasoned, never-been-washed cast-iron skillet to make this bread. Note variations.

2 cups yellow or white cornmeal, preferably
    stoneground (see *Sources*, page 278)

$3/4$ cup all-purpose flour

2 tablespoons sugar

$2 1/2$ teaspoons baking powder

$1/2$ teaspoon baking soda

1 teaspoon salt

2 cups buttermilk

2 large eggs, beaten

$1/4$ cup vegetable oil, preferably sunflower,
    plus additional for the pan

Position a rack in the center of the oven. Generously oil a 9- to 10-inch cast-iron skillet (or a 9-inch cake pan) and place it on the rack. Preheat the oven to 450°F.

Whisk the cornmeal, flour, sugar, baking powder, baking soda, and salt together in a large bowl to combine. Make a well in the center. Whisk the buttermilk, eggs, and oil in another bowl until the eggs are well combined. Pour into the well and stir just until the batter is moistened – do not overbeat.

Remove the hot skillet from the oven and pour in the batter. Bake until the bread springs back when pressed in the center, 15 to 20 minutes. Let stand 5 minutes, then turn out onto a plate or serve directly from the skillet.

Variations

Roasted Tomato, Onions, and Cheddar Cornbread: Heat 2 tablespoons of olive oil in a medium skillet over medium heat. Add 1 coarsely chopped medium onion. Cook, stirring often, until the onion is golden, about 6 minutes. Stir in 2 minced garlic cloves and $1/2$ teaspoon each chopped fresh thyme and oregano, and cook for 1 minute. Cool. Make the batter, stirring just until moistened and lumpy. Stir in the cooled vegetable mixture and $1/2$ cup shredded extra-sharp Cheddar cheese (preferably a farm-style imported British Cheddar). Stir just until smooth. Spread in the hot skillet. Top the batter with 8 Oven-Roasted Tomatoes (page 34). Bake as directed.

Fresh Corn, Chile, and Cheese Cornbread: Preheat the broiler. Broil 1 poblano chile, turning occasionally, until the skin is scorched. Cool. Remove the skin, ribs, and seeds, and chop into $1/2$-inch pieces. Make the batter, stirring just until moistened and lumpy. Stir in the chopped chile, 1 cup fresh corn, cut from the cob, husks reserved, 4 cooked and crumbled bacon strips, $1/2$ cup shredded queso blanco or Monterey Jack cheese, 2 tablespoons of chopped fresh cilantro, and 1 teaspoon of chile powder. Stir just until smooth. Line the hot skillet with corn husks. Pour in batter. Bake as directed.

Boarding House Biscuits

Makes about 14 biscuits

Sometimes I am served biscuits that are so tall, they remind me of a birthday cake. They're okay, but they aren't like the biscuits my grandmother made for me as a kid, the kind that she used to stack in tall heaps at her boarding house. Real biscuits should have a slightly crunchy crust with a soft interior – just like these.

1 cup all-purpose flour

1 cup cake flour

2 teaspoons baking powder

$1/2$ teaspoon baking soda

1 teaspoon salt

4 tablespoons ($1/2$ stick) unsalted butter, cut into $1/2$-inch cubes

$3/4$ cup buttermilk, as needed

Position a rack in the center of the oven and preheat to 400°F.

Whisk the all-purpose flour, cake flour, baking powder, baking soda, and salt in a medium bowl. Using a pastry blender, cut in the butter until the mixture is crumbly with a few pea-size pieces of butter. Stir in enough of the buttermilk to make a soft, sticky dough.

Turn out onto a lightly floured work surface. Quickly knead the dough just until it comes together; do not overknead. Pat or roll out the dough until it is $1/2$-inch thick. Using a $2^1/2$-inch biscuit cutter, cut out biscuits and place 1 inch apart on an ungreased baking sheet. Gather up the scraps, knead briefly, and repeat until all the dough has been used.

Bake until golden brown, about 18 minutes.

Variation

Boarding House Biscuits with Cheddar, Chives, and Pepper: Cut $1/2$ cup grated Cheddar cheese into the flour mixture with the butter. Add 2 tablespoons finely chopped chives and $1/2$ teaspoon coarsely cracked black pepper, then stir in the buttermilk.

No-Knead Dinner Rolls

Makes 2 dozen rolls

My grandmother Mabel is a no-fuss kind of cook. Let other cooks knead and knead the dough for their yeast rolls – Mabel's rolls always turn out light and fluffy and she never kneads them.

2 cups warm (105°F to 115°F) water

Two $1/4$-ounce packages active dry yeast

$1/2$ cup sugar

2 large eggs, beaten

3 tablespoons vegetable oil, plus additional oil for brushing

1 teaspoon salt

6 cups all-purpose flour

3 tablespoons unsalted butter, melted

Pour the water into a large bowl and sprinkle in the yeast. Let stand until the yeast softens, about 5 minutes. Add the sugar, eggs, 3 tablespoons oil, and salt and stir to dissolve the yeast. Gradually stir in enough of the flour to make a soft dough (you may have to use your hands to work in the last additions). Work the dough in the bowl to make a smooth mass.

Lightly brush the top of the dough with additional oil. Cover the bowl tightly with plastic wrap. Let stand in a warm place until doubled in volume, about 1 hour.

Brush two 9- to 10-inch round cake pans with some of the melted butter; reserve the remaining butter. Punch down the dough. Cut the dough into 24 pieces. Form each piece of dough into a smooth ball. Arrange 12 balls of dough, smooth sides up, in each pan. Cover loosely with plastic wrap and let stand in a warm place until puffy and almost doubled in volume, about 35 minutes.

Meanwhile position a rack in the center of the oven and preheat to 400°F. Reheat the reserved butter to melt, if necessary. Brush the tops of the rolls with melted butter. Bake until the rolls are golden brown, about 20 minutes.

Let stand 5 minutes. Unmold and break the rolls apart. Serve hot or warm.

Homemade Corn Tortillas

Makes 12 tortillas

Why make tortillas when you can get them at the store? Because, like so many other edibles, nothing beats homemade. You'll need masa harina, a flour made from slaked dried corn (don't confuse it with cornmeal or plain corn flour), and a tortilla press.

2 cups masa harina

$1/2$ teaspoon salt

1 cup warm water

Whisk together the masa harina and salt in a medium bowl. Gradually stir in the water to form a soft dough. Divide the dough into 12 equal pieces and roll each piece into a ball. Cover the balls with plastic wrap. Let stand for at least 30 and up to 60 minutes.

Place a small plastic sandwich bag on the bottom of a tortilla press. Center a ball of dough on the plastic bag, top with another sandwich bag, and close the press to form a thin tortilla. Remove the top bag, flip the tortilla onto a plate, and remove the other bag. Repeat with all the dough, stacking the tortillas as you make them.

Heat a cast-iron skillet or griddle over medium-high heat. In batches, cook the tortillas until firm, turning once, about $1 1/2$ minutes per side. Wrap the tortillas in a clean kitchen towel to keep warm. Serve hot. (The tortillas can be prepared up to 3 days ahead, cooled, wrapped in plastic, and refrigerated. Reheat, wrapped in aluminum foil, in a 350°F oven for 10 to 15 minutes. Or separate the stacked tortillas with damp paper towels, and microwave on High, allowing about 10 seconds per tortilla.)

Note: Masa harina and tortilla presses are available at Latin grocers or online at www.mexgrocer.com (see Sources, *page 278).*

The Family Meal

When I began my career as a private cook in my twenties, I was fortunate enough to land a job with a family with four adorable daughters, ages thirteen to eighteen.

They, like all teenagers, had their own likes, prejudices, and dislikes, and I had a good time anticipating these. To do this, I relied heavily on what I had learned from the wonderful women who raised me and taught me about the value of family. My mother and grandmother were always there, as was a wise and loving woman named Leila Curry.

When I was small, my father and mother decided to buy my grandmother's farm. This meant that my mother had to go to work. They left my brother and me in the care of Leila. She was not only an accomplished Southern cook – I can still remember exactly how her fried chicken tasted – but a gentle and compassionate companion. I often say today that I had two mothers. Is it possible to be loved too much? I surely was showered with love when I was a child!

My brother Gene and I spent many afternoons on our big old screen porch shelling peas, snapping beans, and husking corn with Leila. I asked her endless questions and always got considered answers. When anti-civil rights violence broke out in nearby states and we watched footage of it on the television news, I asked Leila why people had to hurt each other. "We just have to learn to love each other, honey," she told me, and to this day I still ponder this simple truth. But mostly, on those hot summer days, I remember the feel of the noisy electric fan as it blew slightly cooled, moist air against my legs and arms, adding to that sense of contentment and security experienced by all loved children.

This sense of security is underscored when a family regularly comes together for meals. As a private cook who works in the family home, I have witnessed some tense situations and I can assure you, a good, home-cooked meal has the power to soothe. When I hear laughter erupt in a quiet dining room, I know I am home free. Eating a meal together is almost magical – and creating this magic gets easier the more you do it.

Before any family can sit down to a meal, the cook has to decide what to prepare. Even I, whose profession it is to come up with menus, sometimes have trouble. My best advice is to listen to your family; they will let you know what they like and don't like. In the end, a good meal restores sweetness to life.

Breakfast

Every day is a new beginning, which is why breakfast is the perfect time to sit down for a few minutes and enjoy each other before we face the world. Give yourself time to eat some good, healthful food and to reflect on the day to come.

I recall cold North Florida mornings (if 35 degrees Fahrenheit can be considered cold) when I woke up to the smell of sausage being cooked in a cast-iron pan, which my mother served alongside the best grits in the South. More likely than not, we'd also get a hot biscuit drenched in homemade cane syrup with its rich molasses flavor.

Americans have always had a love affair with breakfast. From Southwestern Huevos Rancheros to Sausage, Egg, and Cheese Pie or thick, golden slices of toasted home-made bread spread with glistening berry jam, we know the right foods to start the day. It's also a good idea to offer a few words of encouragement to each other as we leave the house. My mother used to send me off to school in the morning with the words: "Chin Up!" More than once that phrase has helped me through a day.

Zucchini and Tomato Frittata

Makes 8 servings

Frittata is not only one of the best things you can serve on the brunch table, it makes a great sandwich filling, too. Try it on focaccia with sun-dried tomato pesto (see page 28).

2 tablespoons extra-virgin olive oil

2 medium zucchini, cut into ⅛-inch-thick
   half-moons

1 small Vidalia onion, cut into ⅛-inch-thick
   half-moons

1 garlic clove

2 ripe Roma or plum tomatoes, seeded and
   chopped into 1-inch cubes

8 large eggs

¼ cup (2 ounces) freshly grated
   Parmesan cheese

2 tablespoons minced chives

½ teaspoon salt

¼ teaspoon freshly ground pepper

Position a rack in the center of the oven and preheat to 350°F.

Heat the olive oil in a 10-inch nonstick skillet over medium-high heat. Add the zucchini and cook until softened, about 4 minutes. Add the onion and garlic and cook until the onion softens, about 2 minutes. Stir in the tomato and heat through, about 2 minutes.

Whisk the eggs, Parmesan cheese, chives, salt, and pepper in a large bowl. Pour over the vegetables. Reduce the heat to medium-low. Cook, uncovered, until the bottom of the eggs are set, about 3 minutes. Transfer the skillet to the oven.

Bake until the frittata feels set when pressed in the center, 12 to 15 minutes. Invert onto a serving plate. Serve hot or cooled just to room temperature.

Sausage, Egg, and Cheese Pie

Makes 8 to 10 servings

My Aunt Evelyn makes this every Christmas morning. It resembles a quiche, and like that savory pie, it can be served whenever you want something special for lunch, brunch, or supper.

Perfect Cream Cheese Piecrust (page 203)

1 pound bulk pork sausage

10 large eggs

$1/2$ teaspoon salt

$1/4$ teaspoon freshly ground black pepper

$1/2$ cup (2 ounces) shredded sharp
  Cheddar cheese

Position a rack in the bottom third of the oven and preheat to 350°F.

On a lightly floured surface, roll out the dough into an $1/8$-inch-thick circle. Fold in half, and place in a 9-inch pie pan. Unfold and fit into the pan. Fold the edges of the dough over so they are flush with the edge of the pan and flute the edges. Freeze for 15 minutes.

Cook the sausage in a large skillet over medium-high heat, breaking up the sausage with a spoon, until browned, about 10 minutes. Drain well.

Beat the eggs well with the salt and pepper. Add the sausage and pour into the pie shell. Bake for 30 minutes. Sprinkle the top with the cheese and bake until the cheese melts and a knife inserted in the center of the filling comes out clean, about 15 minutes more. Serve hot.

Baked Eggs with Garden Vegetable Hash

Makes 6 servings

This is one of my favorite breakfast recipes.

$1 1/2$ pounds Yukon Gold potatoes (about 4
  medium), peeled and cut into $1/2$-inch cubes

1 small red bell pepper, cut into $1/2$-inch dice

2 medium zucchini, cut into $1/4$-inch-thick
  half-moons

1 medium yellow onion, cut into $1/2$-inch dice

3 tablespoons extra-virgin olive oil

Salt and freshly ground pepper

1 pound Roma or plum tomatoes, seeded
  and chopped

2 garlic cloves, minced

2 teaspoons chopped fresh thyme

6 large eggs

$1/4$ cup freshly grated Parmesan cheese

Position a rack in the center of the oven and preheat to 450°F. Lightly oil a large baking sheet or roasting pan.

Toss the potatoes, bell pepper, zucchini, onion, and olive oil on the baking sheet and season to taste with salt and pepper. Bake, occasionally turning the vegetables with a spatula, until the potatoes are almost tender, about 40 minutes. Stir in the tomatoes, garlic, and thyme. Bake until the vegetables are browned, about 20 minutes more. Transfer the vegetables to a 2-quart ovenproof serving dish.

Spacing them evenly apart, break the eggs over the vegetables. Bake until the eggs are set, about 10 minutes. Sprinkle with the cheese and serve immediately.

Chicken Strata

Makes 6 to 8 servings

If you want to serve something warm and nourishing for breakfast, but you want a relaxing morning without lots of cooking and cleaning up, the solution is to prepare strata the night before. It is almost like a savory bread pudding. This kind of casserole can be pretty high in fat grams, but I use chicken broth and reduced-fat mayonnaise to trim some of the fat. You need cooked chicken for this strata, so if you're pressed for time, buy a rotisserie-cooked chicken at the supermarket.

1 tablespoon unsalted butter

1 medium onion, finely chopped

3 celery ribs, finely chopped

6 ounces asparagus, woody stems discarded,
   cut into 1-inch pieces

1/4 cup water

4 cups cubed (1-inch cubes) cooked chicken
   (20 ounces)

1 cup mayonnaise, preferably reduced-fat

1 1/2 cups milk

1 1/2 Chicken Broth (page 46) or canned
   low-sodium broth

6 large eggs

1 tablespoon chopped fresh parsley

1 tablespoon chopped fresh chives

1 teaspoon salt

1/2 teaspoon freshly ground black pepper

6 cups cubed (1-inch cubes) French or Italian
   bread (6 ounces)

1 cup (4 ounces) shredded sharp
   Cheddar cheese

Heat the butter in a large skillet over medium heat. Add the onion and celery and cook, uncovered, stirring occasionally, until softened, about 5 minutes. Add the asparagus and water and cover. Cook until the asparagus is crisp-tender, about 3 minutes. Uncover and cook until all liquid is evaporated, about 2 minutes. Transfer the vegetables to a large bowl.

Add the chicken and mayonnaise and mix well. Whisk the milk, broth, eggs, parsley, chives, salt, and pepper in another bowl.

Lightly butter a 13 x 9-inch glass baking dish. Spread half of the bread cubes in the dish, then top with the chicken mixture. Spread the remaining cubes over the chicken. Slowly pour the egg mixture over the ingredients in the dish. Cover and refrigerate for at least 4 hours and up to 10 hours.

Position a rack in the center of the oven and preheat to 350°F.

Bake the strata for 45 minutes. Sprinkle the top with the cheese, and bake until the cheese is melted and a knife inserted in the center comes out clean, about 15 minutes more. Let stand for 5 minutes, then serve hot.

Breakfast is the perfect time to sit down for a few minutes and enjoy each other before we face

the world. Give yourself time to eat some good, healthful food and to reflect on the day to come.

Huevos Rancheros

Makes 6 servings

My chef friend Karen Armijo was cooking in Mexico on a yacht and had brought with her, from California, loaves of challah bread to make French toast. The morning she made it, the food came back to the kitchen uneaten. The daughter came into the galley and asked, "Do you know how to make huevos rancheros?" Ever since then she has been making it wherever she cooks and for all types of families.

Ranchero Sauce

1 tablespoon extra-virgin olive oil

1 medium onion, chopped

3 poblano or Anaheim chiles or cubanelle
   peppers, ribs and seeds removed, cut into
   1/4-inch dice

2 garlic cloves, finely chopped

1 tablespoon pure ground chile powder,
   such as ancho (see *Sources*, page 278)

1 1/2 pounds ripe Roma or plum tomatoes,
   chopped into 1/4-inch dice

1/2 cup Chicken Broth (page 46) or canned
   low-sodium broth

Salt and freshly ground pepper

4 tablespoons extra-virgin olive oil

12 corn tortillas

12 large eggs

Salt and freshly ground pepper

1/2 cup crumbled queso blanco (dry white
   Mexican-style cheese), or use shredded
   Monterey Jack cheese

To make the sauce, heat the oil in a medium saucepan over medium heat. Add the onion and chiles. Cook, stirring occasionally, until the onion is translucent, about 6 minutes. Add the garlic and cook until fragrant, about 1 minute. Stir in the chile powder, then the tomatoes and broth. Bring to a simmer. Reduce the heat to medium-low. Simmer, uncovered, until the sauce thickens, about 30 minutes. Season to taste with salt. (The sauce can be prepared up to 2 days ahead, cooled, covered, and refrigerated. Reheat before using.)

Position racks in the center and top third of the oven and preheat to 200°F.

Heat 2 tablespoons of the oil in a large skillet over high heat until very hot but not smoking. In batches, cook the tortillas, turning once, until crisp and golden, about 1 minute per tortilla. Drain the tortillas on paper towels.

Heat the remaining 2 tablespoons of oil over medium heat. In batches, break the eggs into the skillet and fry them according to your preference. Season to taste with salt and pepper.

For each serving, place 2 tortillas in an individual casserole or on a plate. Top with about 1/2 cup of the sauce, then 2 fried eggs. As each serving is prepared, keep warm in the oven until you are finished. Top each serving with the cheese and serve hot.

Sweet Potato-Pecan Waffles

Makes twelve 4-inch waffles

Sweet potatoes find their way into many Southern baked goods, so it was just a matter of time before I put them into waffles. These cook up moist and flavorful. If you want them the way they eat them in the South, use sorghum syrup instead of maple syrup.

1 1/2 cups all-purpose flour

1/4 cup sugar

1 tablespoon baking powder

1/2 teaspoon ground cinnamon

1/2 teaspoon salt

1 1/2 cups milk

1/2 cup mashed sweet potatoes (see Note)

4 tablespoons (1/2 stick) unsalted butter, melted

3 large eggs, separated, at room temperature

1/3 cup finely chopped pecans

Pure maple syrup or sorghum syrup, for serving

Heat a waffle iron according to the manufacturer's directions. Lightly oil the grids. Meanwhile, whisk the flour, sugar, baking powder, cinnamon, and salt in a large bowl to combine, and make a well in the center. Whisk the milk, sweet potatoes, melted butter, and egg yolks in a medium bowl until well combined and pour into the well. Whisk just until smooth; do not overmix.

Beat the whites in a medium bowl just until stiff peaks begin to form. Stir one-fourth of the whites into the batter to lighten it, then fold in the rest. Fold in the pecans.

Spoon about 1/4 cup of the batter into the center of each quadrant of the waffle iron and close the iron. Cook until the waffle is golden brown, 3 to 4 minutes. Serve the waffles hot, with the syrup passed on the side.

Note: *To cook sweet potatoes, wrap individual sweet potatoes in foil. Bake in a preheated 400°F for 1 hour until tender. Cool completely. Remove the skin and mash the sweet potato flesh with a potato masher or electric mixer. One pound of sweet potatoes will make about 1 cup of mashed.*

Sour Cream Waffles

Makes twelve 4-inch waffles

Sour cream gives baked goods a lighter and delicious texture. These are waffles worth getting out of bed for!

1 3/4 cups all-purpose flour

1 tablespoon sugar

1 tablespoon baking powder

1/2 teaspoon salt

8 tablespoons (1 stick) unsalted butter, melted

1 cup milk

1/2 cup sour cream

3 large eggs

Maple syrup or jam, for serving

Heat a waffle iron according to the manufacturer's directions. Lightly oil the grids. Meanwhile, whisk the flour, sugar, baking powder, and salt in a large bowl to combine and make a well in the center. Whisk the melted butter, milk, sour cream, and eggs in a medium bowl until well combined and pour into the well. Whisk just until smooth; do not overmix.

Spoon about 1/4 cup of the batter into the center of each quadrant of the waffle iron and close the iron. Cook until the waffle is golden brown, 3 to 4 minutes. Serve the waffles hot, with the syrup passed on the side.

Coconut Waffles with Mango-Strawberry Compote

Makes twelve 4-inch waffles

With the flavors of coconut and mango, these waffles take on a tropical note. Let the fruit compote stand at room temperature for at least thirty minutes before serving – you wouldn't want to put cold fruit on hot waffles! Use whatever berries are handy – this is good with raspberries and blueberries, too, or a combination.

Compote

1 ripe mango, peeled, pitted, and cut into
    small cubes

1 pint strawberries, hulled and sliced

1 tablespoon sugar

Waffles

1 3/4 cups all-purpose flour

2 tablespoons sugar

1 tablespoon baking powder

1/2 teaspoon salt

8 tablespoons (1 stick) unsalted butter, melted

1 cup milk

3 large eggs, beaten

1/2 cup coconut milk (not sweetened cream
    of coconut)

1/4 cup shredded sweetened coconut

Fresh mint, for garnish

To make the compote, toss the mango, strawberries, and sugar in a medium bowl. Cover and let stand until the fruit gives off some juices, about 90 minutes.

To make the waffles, heat a waffle iron according to the manufacturer's directions. Lightly oil the grids.

Meanwhile, whisk the flour, sugar, baking powder, and salt in a large bowl to combine. Make a well in the center and pour in the melted butter, milk, eggs, and coconut milk. Whisk just until smooth; do not overmix. Mix in the coconut.

Spoon about 1/4 cup of the batter into the center of each quadrant of the waffle iron and close the iron. Cook until the waffle is golden brown, 3 to 4 minutes.

Serve the waffles hot, spooning the compote on top. Garnish with the mint leaves.

Lemon Pancakes with Raspberry Sauce

Makes 22 to 24 pancakes

This is one of my most requested brunch items. You'll love the tart yet sweet flavor of these pancakes. Dust them with confectioners' sugar and don't forget the fruit sauce. It is a welcome change from maple syrup.

Raspberry Sauce

12 ounces fresh raspberries

1/4 cup granulated sugar

2 teaspoons fresh lemon juice

continued on next page

Lemon Pancakes with Raspberry Sauce continued

Pancakes

$1/2$ cup sour cream

1 tablespoon unsalted butter, melted

1 large egg

1 tablespoon grated lemon zest

$1/2$ cup fresh lemon juice

$1/4$ cup milk, or more as needed

1 cup self-rising flour

2 tablespoons granulated sugar

Confectioners' sugar, for serving

Grated lemon zest, for serving

To make the raspberry sauce, purée the raspberries, sugar, and lemon juice in a food processor or blender. Rub the purée through a wire sieve into a bowl.

To make the pancakes, combine the sour cream, melted butter, egg, lemon zest, lemon juice, and milk in a bowl and beat well. Add the flour and sugar. Stir carefully but do not overmix. Add more milk if the batter is too thick.

Preheat a griddle or nonstick pan. Test with a little batter to see if the griddle is hot. When the griddle is ready, pour silver-dollar-size pancakes. Watch for little bubbles to form on the surface. Cook for 3 to 4 minutes per side. Serve hot, garnished with confectioners' sugar and grated lemon zest.

Jalapeño, Cheddar, and Cornmeal Pancakes

Makes about eighteen $4^1/2$-inch pancakes

These mildly sweetened, savory pancakes would be great with grilled pork sausage or chorizo. Instead of maple syrup, try them with warmed honey to keep the Southwestern flavor. Expect this batter to be quite thin and allow plenty of space between the pancakes for them to spread.

$1^1/4$ cups yellow cornmeal, preferably stoneground

$3/4$ cup all-purpose flour

$1^3/4$ teaspoons baking powder

$3/4$ teaspoon salt

$1/4$ teaspoon pure ground chile powder, such as ancho, or chile powder (see Note)

2 cups milk

$1/4$ cup pure maple syrup

2 large eggs, beaten

3 tablespoons unsalted butter, melted

$1/2$ cup (2 ounces) shredded sharp Cheddar or jalapeño Jack cheese

1 jalapeño chile, seeded and minced

2 tablespoons finely chopped fresh cilantro

Maple syrup or honey, for serving

Heat a griddle until a splash of water immediately forms tiny balls that skitter over the surface. Lightly oil the griddle.

Meanwhile, whisk the cornmeal, flour, baking powder, salt, and chile powder in a large bowl to combine. Make a well in the center, and pour in the milk, maple syrup, eggs, and melted butter. Whisk just until smooth (the batter will be thin). Mix in the cheese, minced jalapeño, and cilantro.

Using ¼ cup of batter for each pancake and spacing the pancakes well apart (the batter will spread), spoon the batter onto the griddle. Cook just until the undersides are golden and the tops of the pancakes are covered with tiny holes, about 2 minutes. Flip the pancakes and cook until the other sides are golden. Serve hot, with the maple syrup or honey.

Note: *Pure ground chiles are pulverized dried chiles without any additional seasoning. Chiles have different flavors and levels of heat – ancho is relatively mild, but chipotle will be very hot. You can find pure ground chile powder at Latin markets, specialty grocers, and some supermarkets, or by mail order (see* Sources, *page 278). Chile powder, used to flavor a pot of Texas-style chile, combines ground chiles with other seasonings like oregano, ground cumin, and garlic powder, and can be found at any supermarket.*

Sesame Orange Granola

Makes about 8 cups

This cereal is a great way to start your morning. Serve it over yogurt with fresh fruit and you will feel energized until lunch. You can double the batch and keep it sealed in an airtight container for a few months.

1 cup sweetened shredded coconut

½ cup vegetable oil

⅓ cup maple syrup

Grated zest of 2 large oranges

4 cups old-fashioned (rolled) oats

1 cup (4 ounces) sliced almonds

1 cup (4 ounces) coarsely chopped unsalted
   cashews

⅓ cup honey

2 teaspoons ground cinnamon

½ teaspoon freshly grated nutmeg

⅓ cup sesame seeds

1 cup chopped dried fruit, such as dates, apples,
   or apricots, or a combination

Position racks in the center and upper third of the oven and preheat to 375°F.

Spread the coconut on a baking sheet. Bake on the center rack, stirring often, until lightly toasted, about 10 minutes. Transfer to a large bowl.

Bring the oil, maple syrup, and orange zest to a boil over medium heat in a medium saucepan. Place the oats, almonds, cashews, honey, cinnamon, nutmeg, and sesame seeds in the bowl of a heavy-duty mixer and mix on low speed with the paddle attachment until combined, about 1 minute (or mix well with your hands in a large bowl). Add the syrup mixture and mix (or toss with 2 large spoons) until well coated. Spread in ½-inch-thick layers on 2 large baking sheets.

Bake, stirring often, switching the positions of the baking sheets from top to bottom and front to back halfway through baking, until the granola is golden brown, about 15 minutes.

Remove from the oven and let cool. Stir into the bowl of coconut along with the dried fruit. (The granola can be stored at room temperature in airtight containers for up to 1 month.)

Maple, Walnut, and Thyme Muffins

Makes 12 muffins

The addition of fresh thyme to this muffin is a lovely surprise. The earthy combination of nuts and herbs makes this a wonderful treat to enjoy any time of day.

1^3/4 cups all-purpose flour

2 teaspoons baking powder

1 teaspoon baking soda

^{1}/4 teaspoon salt

8 tablespoons (1 stick) unsalted butter,
    at room temperature

^{3}/4 cup pure maple syrup

1 cup sour cream

1 large egg

^{1}/2 cup chopped walnuts

2 tablespoons chopped fresh thyme

Position a rack in the center of the oven and preheat to 400°F. Lightly butter and flour twelve 2^1/2-inch muffin cups. Tap out excess flour.

Whisk the flour, baking powder, baking soda, and salt in a medium bowl to combine. In another medium bowl, using a hand-held electric mixer on high speed, beat the butter until creamy, about 1 minute. Gradually beat in the maple syrup, then add the sour cream and egg. Add the flour mixture and stir just until blended. Fold in the walnuts and thyme. Spoon equal amounts of the batter into the muffin cups, filling them about three-fourths full.

Bake until a toothpick inserted in the center of a muffin comes out clean, 15 to 20 minutes. Cool in the pan for 5 minutes. Remove the muffins and serve warm, or cool on a wire rack.

Mixed Berry Muffins

Makes 12 muffins

This is a straightforward muffin recipe. Prepare the dry ingredients the night before in a zippered plastic bag. In the morning mix in the wet ingredients and smell them baking while you drink your first cup of coffee.

2 cups all-purpose flour

$^3/4$ cup sugar

$2^1/2$ teaspoons baking powder

$^1/4$ teaspoon baking soda

$^1/4$ teaspoon salt

1 cup milk

$^1/2$ cup vegetable oil

2 large eggs

$1^1/3$ cups fresh berries, such as blueberries, raspberries, blackberries, huckleberries, or sliced strawberries, or a combination

Position a rack in the center of the oven and preheat to 400°F. Lightly butter twelve $2^1/2$-inch muffin cups.

In a medium bowl, whisk the flour, sugar, baking powder, baking soda, and salt to combine and make a well in the center. In another medium bowl, whisk the milk, oil, and eggs. Mix well and pour into the well. Stir just until blended. Fold in the berries. Spoon equal amounts of the batter into the muffin cups, filling them about three-fourths full.

Bake until a toothpick inserted in the center of a muffin comes out clean, 15 to 20 minutes. Cool in the pan for 5 minutes. Remove the muffins and serve warm or cool on a wire rack.

Lunch

The world is a crazy place, and there are days when we're too busy for lunch. If I have had a good breakfast, I can usually get by with a piece of fruit for lunch, but I would rather not resort to this.

In the South we call lunch dinner, and dinner is called supper. Dinner in rural parts of the region is generally a large meal, very welcome after a long, hard morning, and necessary to nourish farmers for the afternoon ahead. Supper is lighter.

Today, in most of the country, lunch is a relatively light meal. One of the best I know is soup and a simple salad. A good soup can be made ahead of time, portioned into containers, and frozen. These can be reheated either in your own kitchen or at your place of work. Soup can also be shared with shut-ins and the elderly, and that is why when I make it, I always make a lot. If you pair the soup with a small salad of fresh greens tossed with a light dressing, such as Ice Box Buttermilk Dressing, you have a meal to see you happily through until dinnertime.

Lunch is also a good opportunity to meet friends and associates who, while not part of our inner families, add richness and depth to our lives. Even sitting down to eat lunch in a restaurant is reviving. Portions tend to be enormous, so don't hesitate to split one with your lunch partner. This is just another way to share our meal and our connection with each other at the table.

Oxtail Soup with Barley and Mushrooms

Makes 8 servings

For homemade beef soup, there is hardly a better choice than oxtails. Their flavorful meat and abundance of bones provide the beginnings of a great broth. Barley and fresh mushrooms add even more sustenance. You can use just about any kind of dried mushroom. For this soup, generic dried mushrooms from Poland or Argentina will be just fine.

1 cup (about 1^1/$_2$ ounces) dried mushrooms, rinsed under cold water to remove grit

1 cup boiling water

3 pounds oxtails, cut into 2-inch chunks by the butcher

Salt and freshly ground black pepper

^{1}/$_3$ cup all-purpose flour

4 tablespoons extra-virgin olive oil, plus more as needed

1 large onion, chopped

2 celery ribs, chopped

2 medium carrots, chopped into ^{1}/$_2$-inch slices

1 pound cremini mushrooms, thinly sliced

2 garlic cloves, minced

1^1/$_2$ quarts water, or as needed

4 sprigs fresh thyme, or 1 teaspoon dried thyme

1 bay leaf

^{1}/$_2$ cup pearl barley

Chopped fresh parsley, for garnish

Soak the dried mushrooms in the boiling water in a small bowl until the mushrooms soften, about 20 minutes. Strain through a wire sieve lined with a dampened paper towel, reserving the liquid.

Season the oxtails with salt and pepper to taste. Place the flour in a shallow dish. Roll the oxtails in the flour to coat and shake off the excess flour. Heat 2 tablespoons of the oil in a large soup pot over medium-high heat. In batches, add the oxtails and cook, turning occasionally, until browned, about 8 minutes. Transfer the oxtails to a plate.

Wipe out the pot with paper towels. Heat the remaining 2 tablespoons of oil in the pot over medium heat. Add the onion, celery, and carrots and cook until the vegetables soften, about 10 minutes. Add the sliced mushrooms and garlic and cook until the mushrooms are wilted, about 5 minutes.

Return the oxtails to the pot. Add the soaked mushrooms and the strained liquid, with enough water to cover the ingredients by 1 inch. Bring to a boil over high heat, skimming off any foam that rises to the surface. Add the thyme and bay leaf. Reduce the heat to medium-low. Simmer, partially covered, for 2 hours. Add the barley and continue cooking until the meat and barley are tender, about 1 hour more.

Remove the pot from the heat and let stand 5 minutes. Skim off any fat that rises to the surface (there could be quite a bit, as oxtails are fatty). Season to taste with salt and pepper.

Ladle into soup bowls, sprinkling each serving with parsley.

Green Pea Soup with Little Vegetables

Makes 8 servings

This is a soup that was inspired by my friend Susan Weaver. It is a gorgeous, emerald-green soup, with a hearty vegetable flavor that is warming but not too filling. It makes a fine chilled soup, too.

Vegetable Garnish

1 cup fresh or frozen green peas

1 cup asparagus tips

1 cup finely diced carrots

Green Pea Soup

2 tablespoons extra-virgin olive oil

1 medium onion, chopped

2 celery ribs, chopped

2 garlic cloves, minced

1 medium Yukon Gold potato, peeled and
   finely chopped (1 cup)

6 cups Vegetable Broth (page 46), Chicken
   Broth (page 46), or canned low-sodium broth

4 cups fresh or frozen green peas, rinsed
   under cold water

1 large bunch watercress, stemmed (about
   1 1/2 cups packed leaves)

2 tablespoons fresh lemon juice

Salt and freshly ground black pepper

Chopped fresh mint, for garnish

To prepare the vegetable garnish, bring a medium saucepan of lightly salted water to a boil. Add the peas and cook just until tender, about 5 minutes for fresh peas, 2 minutes for frozen. Drain and rinse under cold water to stop the cooking. (If you have a large skimmer, you can fish out the peas and keep the water boiling.) Transfer the peas to bowl.

Repeat with the asparagus, cooking just until crisp-tender, about 4 minutes, rinse, and add to the bowl. Repeat with the carrots, cooking just until crisp-tender, about 3 minutes, rinse, and add to the bowl. (The vegetables can be prepared up to 3 hours ahead, covered, and kept at room temperature.)

To make the soup, heat the oil in a soup pot over medium heat. Add the onion and celery and cook, stirring often, until the onion is translucent, about 5 minutes. Add the garlic and cook for 1 minute more. Stir in the potato, then the broth. Bring to a boil over high heat. Reduce the heat to low. Simmer, partially covered, until the potatoes are very tender, about 15 minutes.

Stir in the peas and return to a boil over high heat. Cook until very tender, about 8 minutes for fresh peas and 5 minutes for frozen. Stir in the watercress. In batches, purée in a blender or food processor. Add the lemon juice and season to taste with salt and pepper. Return to the pot and reheat over medium heat until piping hot.

Ladle into soup bowls, and add a spoonful of the vegetable garnish to each serving. Sprinkle with mint and serve.

Lunch is also a good opportunity to meet friends and associates who, while not part of our families, add richness and depth to our lives.

Grilled Tomato and Vegetable Soup

Makes 8 servings

I created this soup one late summer day when we had an abundance of tomatoes and peppers.

3 pounds large ripe tomatoes, cut in half crosswise

6 medium red bell peppers, cut in half lengthwise, ribs and seeds removed

2 medium Vidalia onions, cut in half crosswise, unpeeled

1 large ear corn, unhusked

1 medium head of garlic, wrapped in aluminum foil

4 teaspoons chopped fresh basil

4 teaspoons chopped fresh chives

4 teaspoons chopped fresh oregano

1 quart Chicken Broth (page 46) or canned low-sodium broth

Salt and freshly ground black pepper

Build a fire in a charcoal grill and let burn until the coals are covered with white ash. Or preheat a gas grill on High. Lightly oil the grill grid.

Place the tomatoes, red peppers, onions, corn, and garlic on the grill and cover. Grill the tomatoes, turning occasionally, until lightly charred on both sides, about 5 minutes. Remove from the grill and place in a large bowl. Cool, then discard the peels and seeds.

Grill the peppers, skin side down, until the skin is charred and blistered, about 10 minutes. Remove and cool, then peel.

Grill the onions, cut side down, until grill marks appear, about 5 minutes. Turn right side up and place on the cooler, outer perimeter of the grill grid. Grill until the onions are tender, about 15 minutes. Remove and cool, then discard the onion skin and coarsely chop.

Grill the corn, turning occasionally, until the husk is charred, about 20 minutes. Remove and cool, then pull off the husk and silk. Cut the kernels from the cob.

Grill the packet of garlic, turning often, until it feels tender when squeezed, about 25 minutes. Remove and unwrap. Cool, then cut in half with a serrated knife and squeeze out the flesh.

In a food processor, pulse the tomatoes, peppers, onions, corn, and garlic to make a coarse purée.

Combine the basil, chives, and oregano. In a soup pot, combine the vegetable purée with the broth and 6 teaspoons of the herbs, reserving the remaining herbs for garnish. Cook, stirring often, just until simmering. Season to taste with salt and pepper.

Ladle into soup bowls, sprinkling each serving with the reserved herbs. Serve hot. Or cool completely, then refrigerate until chilled, and serve cold.

Seafood Gumbo

Makes 8 to 12 servings

Gumbo, here made with turkey kielbasa instead of Andouille sausages, can be considered a hearty meal. Gumbo is often made with a roux that is cooked for quite a while on the stove. I find that toasting the flour in a skillet is a great time-saver, with no compromise in flavor.

$1/2$ cup all-purpose flour

3 tablespoons extra-virgin olive oil

2 large onions, chopped

2 celery ribs, chopped

1 small green bell pepper, seeded and chopped

2 garlic cloves, minced

5 cups Chicken Broth (page 46) or canned
   low-sodium broth

1 pound sliced smoked turkey kielbasa,
   cut into $1/2$-inch half-moons

One 14-ounce can stewed tomatoes

1 teaspoon dried thyme

1 teaspoon dried basil

1 teaspoon dried oregano

2 bay leaves

1 pound firm, white-fleshed fish fillets, such as
   snapper or cod, cut into 1-inch chunks

1 pound medium shrimp, peeled and deveined

2 cups cooked chicken cut into bite-size pieces
   (optional)

Salt and freshly ground pepper

Hot red pepper sauce

Chopped scallions, for garnish

Heat an empty skillet over medium heat. Add the flour and cook, stirring constantly, until the flour is fragrant and golden brown but not scorched, about 5 minutes. Transfer the flour to a bowl and set aside.

Heat the oil in a soup pot over medium heat. Add the onions, celery, bell pepper, and garlic. Cook, stirring often, until the vegetables soften, about 10 minutes. Add the flour and stir well. Gradually stir in the broth, then the kielbasa, tomatoes, thyme, basil, oregano, and bay leaves. Bring to a boil over high heat. Reduce the heat to medium-low. Simmer, uncovered, until lightly thickened, about 25 minutes.

Stir in the fish and cook for 5 minutes. Add the shrimp and chicken, if using, and cook until the shrimp and fish are firm, about 3 minutes. Season to taste with salt, pepper, and hot sauce. Serve hot, sprinkling each serving with scallions.

Zucchini, Potato, and Parmesan Soup

A perfect, hearty summer soup.

Makes 8 to 10 servings

1 tablespoon extra-virgin olive oil

1 medium onion, finely chopped

2 celery ribs, finely chopped

3 garlic cloves, minced

3 medium zucchini, scrubbed but unpeeled, cut into $1/2$-inch cubes (4 cups)

1 medium Yukon Gold potato, peeled and cut into $1/2$-inch cubes (1 cup)

3 cups Chicken Broth (page 46) or canned low sodium canned broth, as needed

1 sprig of fresh thyme

1 cup evaporated skimmed milk

3 tablespoons freshly grated Parmesan cheese, plus additional for serving

Salt and freshly ground black pepper

Chopped fresh thyme, for garnish

Heat the oil in a large pot over medium heat. Add the onion, celery, and garlic, and cover. Cook, stirring often, until the onions are translucent, about 5 minutes.

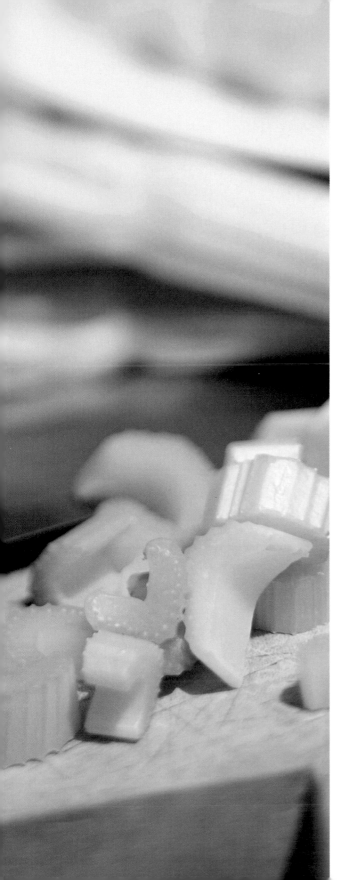

Stir in the zucchini and potato. Add enough broth to barely cover the vegetables. Add the thyme and bring to a boil over high heat. Reduce the heat to low. Simmer, partially covered, until the potato is tender, about 15 minutes.

Stir in the evaporated milk and cheese. Heat until very hot, but do not boil, or the soup will curdle. Season to taste with salt and pepper.

Ladle into soup bowls, and sprinkle each serving with thyme. Pass extra Parmesan cheese on the side. Serve hot.

Carrot-Ginger Soup with Minted Yogurt

Makes 6 to 8 servings

The bright orange color of this soup will provide color to your table as well as please your guests' appetites. The combination of sweet carrots, hot-spicy ginger, and cool mint works well together.

2 tablespoons unsalted butter

1 large onion, chopped

1 1/2 pounds carrots (about 10 medium), peeled and sliced

3 tablespoons peeled and finely chopped fresh ginger

2 garlic cloves, minced

5 cups Vegetable Broth (page 46), Chicken Broth (page 46), or canned low-sodium broth

1 sprig of fresh thyme or 1/4 teaspoon dried thyme

continued on next page

Carrot-Ginger Soup with Minted Yogurt continued

1/4 teaspoon freshly ground pepper,
   or more to taste

1 bay leaf, dried or fresh

1/2 cup milk, whole or reduced-fat

Salt

1 cup plain unflavored yogurt, at room
   temperature

2 tablespoons chopped mint or other fresh
   herbs, such as chives, thyme, tarragon,
   or dill, or a combination

Melt the butter in a soup pot over medium heat.
Add the onion, cover tightly and cook, stirring
often, until the onion is golden, about 6 minutes.
Stir in the carrots, ginger, and garlic and cook for
2 minutes. Stir in the broth, thyme, pepper, and
bay leaf. Bring to a boil over high heat.

Reduce the heat to medium-low. Simmer, partially covered, until the carrots are very tender,
about 20 minutes. Remove the thyme sprig
and bay leaf.

In batches, purée the vegetables and liquid in a
blender or food processor. Pour the soup back
into the pot and stir in the milk. Season to taste
with salt and additional pepper and reheat over
medium heat until piping hot.

Ladle into soup bowls and top each serving with
a dollop of the yogurt and a sprinkling of mint
or other herbs.

Vegetable-Grain Soup

Makes about 12 servings

*Before I make this filling vegetarian soup, I look in the
cupboard to check for small amounts of grains or legumes
I might want to use up, and I toss them into the soup. So
even though this recipe calls for equal amounts of split
peas, barley, and lentils, feel free to substitute one cup of
any dried legumes or grains you have on hand that
sound good to you.*

2 quarts Vegetable Broth (page 46)

1 quart water

1 small onion, coarsely chopped

2 medium carrots, cut into 12-inch-thick rounds

2 celery ribs, cut into 1/2-inch-thick slices

One 14 1/2-ounce can tomatoes with juice

2 garlic cloves, minced

2 sprigs of fresh thyme or 1/2 teaspoon
   dried thyme

1/4 celery root, peeled and cut
   into 1-inch cubes (2 cups)

1/3 cup pearl barley

1/3 cup split peas

1/3 cup lentils, preferably tiny French
   lentilles de Puy

1/4 small head chopped green cabbage
   (about 2 cups)

1 large Yukon Gold potato, peeled and
   cut into 1/2-inch cubes

1 medium zucchini, scrubbed and
   cut into 1/2-inch cubes

1 yellow squash, scrubbed and cut into
$^1/_2$-inch cubes

Salt and freshly ground pepper

Chopped fresh herbs, such as basil, parsley,
or chives, for garnish

Bring the broth, water, onion, carrots, celery,
tomatoes, garlic, and thyme to a boil over
high heat. Reduce the heat to low and simmer
for 1 hour.

Add the celery root, barley, split peas, and lentils
and cook for 40 minutes.

Add the cabbage, potato, zucchini, and squash.
Simmer until all of the ingredients are tender,
about 40 minutes. Remove and discard the thyme
sprigs. Season to taste with salt and pepper.

Serve hot, ladled into soup bowls and sprinkled
with herbs.

Spicy Winter Squash Soup

Makes 8 to 10 servings

*The vibrant flavors of the Caribbean influence this
soup. Any winter squash will do – calabaza, butternut,
or Hubbard squash – or a cooking pumpkin, such as a
sugar pumpkin. Calabaza and plantains are available
at Latin markets. If you can't find green plantains,
use a hard green banana.*

2 tablespoons extra-virgin olive oil

1 large sweet onion, such as Vidalia, chopped

3 celery ribs, chopped

4 garlic cloves, minced

1 tablespoon Madras-style curry powder

$1^1/_2$ pounds butternut squash, pared with a
sharp knife

2 green plantains, peeled and cut up

6 cups Chicken Broth (page 46) or canned
low-sodium broth, as needed

2 sprigs of fresh oregano or $^1/_2$ teaspoon
dried oregano

2 sprigs of fresh sage or $^1/_2$ teaspoon dried sage

$^1/_2$ teaspoon hot red pepper sauce

Salt and freshly ground black pepper

$^1/_4$ cup toasted pumpkin seeds, for garnish

Chopped fresh chives, for garnish

Heat the oil in a soup pot over medium-low
heat. Add the onion and celery and cover. Cook,
stirring occasionally, until the onion is translucent, about 8 minutes. Add the garlic and cook
for 1 minute.

Add the curry powder and stir until fragrant,
about 30 seconds. Stir in the squash and plantain,
then the broth, oregano, and sage. Bring to a boil
over high heat. Reduce the heat to low. Simmer,
partially covered, until the squash is very tender,
about 20 minutes. Remove from the heat.

In batches, pulse the soup in a blender or food
processor to make a chunky purée. Return to the
pot and season to taste with the hot sauce and
salt and pepper. Reheat until piping hot.

Ladle into soup bowls and garnish with the
pumpkin seeds and chives.

Romaine with Lemon-Parmesan Vinaigrette

Makes 4 to 6 servings

Crisp romaine lettuce hearts work well with this creamy Caesar-like dressing.

Lemon-Parmesan Vinaigrette

1 tablespoon mayonnaise

$1/4$ cup (1 ounce) grated Parmesan cheese

3 tablespoons fresh lemon juice

1 teaspoon Worcestershire sauce

$1/4$ cup extra-virgin olive oil

Salt and freshly ground pepper

1 package romaine hearts, torn into
   bite-size pieces

1 ripe Hass avocado, peeled, pitted, and sliced

1 small red bell pepper, seeded and finely diced

1 medium cucumber, cut lengthwise, seeded,
   and cut into thin half-moons

To make the vinaigrette, place the mayonnaise, cheese, lemon juice, and Worcestershire sauce in a blender or food processor. With the machine running, slowly add the olive oil in a steady stream until the dressing thickens. Season to taste with salt and pepper.

Combine the romaine, avocado, bell pepper, and cucumber in a large bowl. Add the vinaigrette and toss to coat evenly. Serve immediately.

Chopped Grilled Vegetable Salad with Yogurt Cucumber Dressing

Makes 6 to 8 servings

You've gone shopping to the local farmer's market, and you realize that your eyes were bigger than your refrigerator. When I have too many vegetables, I grill them for a salad. The more vegetables, the better, so feel free to expand on the ones I suggest here. Sometimes I sprinkle the salad with pumpkin seeds, chopped sun-dried tomatoes, and a grating of fresh Parmesan.

Dressing

1 cup nonfat plain yogurt

$1/2$ cup buttermilk

1 tablespoon Dijon mustard

2 tablespoons balsamic vinegar, preferably
   white balsamic

1 garlic clove, crushed through a press

1 large cucumber, peeled, seeded, grated, and
   squeezed to remove excess moisture

2 tablespoons chopped fresh chives

Salt and freshly ground black pepper

Pinch of cayenne

$1/4$ cup extra-virgin olive oil, for brushing the
   vegetables (or olive oil in a spray bottle)

1 pound asparagus, trimmed

2 medium zucchini, cut lengthwise into
   $1/2$-inch-thick slices

1 medium yellow squash, cut lengthwise into
   $1/2$-inch-thick slices

1 medium globe eggplant or 2 medium
   Japanese eggplants, cut lengthwise into
   $3/4$-inch-thick slices

2 medium red bell peppers or use 1 red and
  1 yellow pepper, tops and bottoms trimmed,
  flesh opened into one long strip, ribs and
  seeds removed

Salt and freshly ground black pepper

4 cups assorted salad greens, preferably a combination of baby spinach, stemmed watercress,
  Bibb lettuce, and Belgian endive leaves

1 pint grape tomatoes

Chopped fresh chives, for garnish

To make the dressing, process the yogurt, butter-milk, mustard, vinegar, and garlic in a food processor until smooth. Add the cucumber and chives and pulse to combine. Season to taste with salt, pepper, and cayenne. Cover and refrigerate. (The dressing can be made up to 2 days ahead, covered, and refrigerated.)

Build a charcoal fire in an outdoor grill and let it burn until the coals are covered with white ashes. For a gas grill, preheat on High. Lightly oil the grill grate.

Brush the asparagus, zucchini, yellow squash, and eggplant with the oil (or spray with oil in a spray bottle). In batches, grill the vegetables, removing them from the grill as they are cooked. Place the asparagus on the grill across the grill grate so they don't fall through the grate. Grill, rolling the asparagus on the grill to turn, until crisp-tender, about 5 minutes, depending on the size of the spears. Grill the zucchini, yellow squash, and eggplant, turning once, until tender, about 8 minutes. Grill the peppers until the skin is charred and blistered, about 10 minutes. Cool, then peel.

Cool the vegetables. Chop into bite-size pieces and season to taste with salt and pepper. You may keep the vegetables separate, or mix them together.

To serve, arrange the greens on a large platter. Arrange the vegetables in separate mounds on the greens (or mound the mixed vegetables in the center). Surround with the tomatoes and sprinkle with chives. Serve immediately, with the dressing passed on the side.

Green Bean Salad with Tomatoes and Feta

Makes 4 to 6 servings

Serve this as a side dish at a cookout or as a light salad for lunch. I think the tomatoes give the salad plenty of acidity, but add a splash of red wine vinegar, if you wish.

1 1/2 pounds green beans, washed and trimmed

1/2 pint grape tomatoes

1/2 cup crumbled feta cheese

1 small shallot, thinly sliced

2 tablespoons chopped fresh mint

2 tablespoons chopped fresh basil

3 tablespoons extra-virgin olive oil

Salt and freshly ground pepper

continued on next page

Green Bean Salad with Tomatoes and Feta continued

Bring a pot of lightly salted water to a boil over high heat. Add the green beans and cook until barely tender, about 5 minutes. Drain and rinse with cold water. Pat the green beans dry with paper towels.

Toss the green beans, tomatoes, feta, shallot, mint, and basil together in a large bowl. Drizzle with the olive oil and season to taste with salt and pepper. Serve immediately.

Fennel, Watercress, and Orange Salad with Citrus Vinaigrette

Makes 4 servings

Serve this salad in the winter, when fennel and oranges are at their peak. Tender mâche greens are a good substitute if the peppery taste of watercress is overwhelming to you.

2 large navel oranges

1 large bulb fennel (about 14 ounces), trimmed of stalks and fronds

2 tablespoons extra-virgin olive oil

2 tablespoons fresh lemon juice

Salt and freshly ground black pepper

Citrus Vinaigrette

1 tablespoon fresh lemon juice

1 tablespoon fresh orange juice, reserved from cutting orange segments

1/4 cup extra-virgin olive oil

Salt and freshly ground pepper

2 large bunches watercress, stemmed, washed, and dried (about 3 cups packed leaves)

Cut off the top and bottom ends of the oranges. Stand an orange on one end and slice off the rind where it meets the flesh. Repeat with the second orange. Run a knife along the membranes that separate each section, pull off the orange segments, and set aside in a small bowl. Squeeze the membranes over a small bowl to extract the orange juice. Set aside 1 tablespoon of the juice and discard the rest.

Cut the fennel in half lengthwise and cut out the hard core. Slice the fennel crosswise into 1/4-inch-thick slices. Heat the olive oil in a large skillet over high heat. Add the fennel slices and cook, without stirring, until the undersides are lightly browned, about 2 minutes. Stir in the lemon juice and cook until the fennel is crisp-tender, about 1 minute. Season to taste with salt and pepper. Transfer to a dish and cool.

To make the vinaigrette, whisk together the lemon and orange juices in a medium bowl. Slowly whisk in the olive oil. Season to taste with salt and pepper.

Combine the fennel, orange segments, and 2 tablespoons of the vinaigrette in a medium bowl. Toss gently and season with salt and pepper. Toss the watercress with the remaining vinaigrette and season to taste with salt and pepper. Place equal amounts of the watercress on 4 plates and top with the fennel-orange mixture. Serve immediately.

Bibb Lettuce Salad with Pecans, Blue Cheese, and Pears

Serves 6

This salad is about the interplay of crisp, sweet pecans with salty, pungent blue cheese, tender greens, and juicy pears. It's all held together with one of my favorite dressings.

1 cup pecan halves

1 tablespoon light corn syrup

1 tablespoon honey

4 small heads Bibb lettuce, washed, dried, and
torn into bite-size pieces

6 tablespoons Late Harvest Riesling Dressing
(page 35)

Salt and freshly ground pepper

3 ounces blue cheese, such as Maytag, crumbled

2 ripe Anjou pears, peeled, cored, and cut into
matchstick-size pieces

Position a rack in the center of the oven and preheat to 350°F.

Spread the pecans on a sheet pan and bake until heated, about 5 minutes. Stir together the corn syrup and honey in a small bowl. Pour the syrup over the nuts and toss to coat evenly. Bake until the nuts have absorbed most of the syrup and are glazed, about 5 minutes. Remove from the oven and cool slightly. Separate the pecans that are sticking together and cool completely.

Toss the lettuce with the dressing in a large bowl and season to taste with salt and pepper. Divide among 6 plates. Sprinkle equal amounts of the cheese, pears, and nuts over the top of each salad. Serve immediately.

Mixed Herbs and Baby Lettuces with Balsamic Vinaigrette

Makes 6 servings

Almost every supermarket now carries bags of mixed baby lettuces and greens, washed and ready for a fine vinaigrette. Keep the leaves whole or torn into pieces, but do not chop them. This is my favorite combination of herbs, but you can use whatever seems good to you.

Balsamic Vinaigrette

3 tablespoons balsamic vinegar

2 tablespoons minced shallot

3 tablespoons extra-virgin olive oil

10 ounces mixed baby lettuces

$1/2$ cup fresh flat-leaf parsley leaves

$1/4$ cup fresh mint leaves

$1/4$ cup fresh tarragon leaves

Scant $1/4$ cup fresh basil leaves, torn into
    small pieces

$1/4$ cup unsprayed edible flowers, such as johnny-
    jump-ups, pansies, or nasturtiums (optional)

1 cup grape tomatoes or Sweet 100
    cherry tomatoes

Salt and freshly ground black pepper

To make the vinaigrette, whisk the vinegar and shallot in a small bowl. Gradually whisk in the oil. Set aside.

Toss the lettuce, parsley, mint, tarragon, basil, and flowers, if using, in a large bowl. Add the vinaigrette and toss again.

To serve, heap the salad in the center of 6 plates. Arrange the tomatoes around the salad. Sprinkle each salad with salt and pepper to taste.

115

Dinner

Wherever we are in this world, at the end of the day we come home to our personal sanctuary for dinner. Without doubt, everyone can relate to the end-of-the-day quandary about what to eat. The advice I have given to others time and again is this: Listen to your family and listen to your heart. It energizes me to fulfill special requests from family members; I know how pleased they will be when they see their heart's desire appear on the dinner table. This doesn't have to be fancy – a piece of baked fish or Mashed Potato Casserole may fit the bill.

When I was growing up, every few weeks my parents loaded Gene and me into the car and drove twenty miles to the nearest hamburger joint. The burgers and fries tasted unbelievable to us, munched from greasy paper bags, but I know that they would have slipped into the realm of the mediocre had we done this more often.

Kids love special meals like this, so if yours have cravings for cheeseburgers, shakes, pizza, or tacos, indulge them now and again but try to get the food to go. Eat it around the dining room table where you can share conversation and a few filched French fries, not in the backseat of the car!

Gathering at the table at day's end is a far superior method of communication than beepers, cell phones, e-mail, and videos. Plain old conversation is still the best way to enjoy each other, and suppertime is a chance to celebrate being a family and to count our blessings.

Baked Crab Cakes with Spicy Remoulade Sauce

Makes 4 servings

Crab cakes make a quick, but elegant, supper – all you need is good crab. They're often panfried, but I much prefer to bake them. Every coastal region of the country has a special variety of crabmeat, from blue crab (my favorite) to Dungeness. To reduce calories, use store-bought reduced-fat mayonnaise and sour cream.

Remoulade Sauce

1 cup Homemade Mayonnaise (page 32)
   or use store-bought mayonnaise

3 tablespoons grainy mustard, such as Creole
   or moutarde de Meaux

3 tablespoons sour cream

1 tablespoon seeded and finely chopped green
   or red bell pepper

1 tablespoon peeled, seeded, and finely
   chopped cucumber

1 tablespoon minced capers

1 tablespoon chopped fresh parsley

1/4 teaspoon hot red pepper sauce, or more
   to taste

Freshly ground black pepper

Crab Cakes

Nonstick cooking oil spray

1 tablespoon extra-virgin olive oil

1 medium onion, finely chopped

2 celery ribs, finely chopped

1 small green or red bell pepper, seeded and
   finely chopped

1 jalapeño pepper, seeded and minced

2 garlic cloves, minced

1/2 cup Homemade Mayonnaise (page 32)
   or use store-bought mayonnaise

2 tablespoons chopped fresh parsley

1 tablespoon Dijon mustard

1 tablespoon Old Bay Seasoning

1 large egg or 2 large egg whites, beaten

1 pound crabmeat, picked over for cartilage

1 cup dried breadcrumbs

To make the remoulade sauce, stir all of the ingredients in a small bowl, using plenty of hot sauce and pepper. Cover and refrigerate for at least 1 hour for the flavors to blend. (The sauce can be prepared up to 3 days ahead, covered, and refrigerated.)

To make the crab cakes, position a rack in the top third of the oven and preheat to 375°F. Lightly spray a baking sheet with cooking oil spray.

Heat the olive oil in a large nonstick skillet over medium heat. Add the onion, celery, bell pepper, jalapeño, and garlic and cook, stirring often, until tender, about 10 minutes. Remove from the heat and cool completely.

Mix the mayonnaise, parsley, mustard, seasoning, and egg to combine. Add the crabmeat and 1/4 cup of the breadcrumbs and mix lightly just until combined. Form the mixture into 8 cakes. Place the remaining breadcrumbs in a shallow dish and dredge the cakes in them. Arrange the cakes on the baking sheet and spray with cooking oil spray.

Bake 10 minutes. Carefully turn the cakes and spray again with oil. Bake until the cakes are crisp, about 10 minutes more. Serve hot, with the remoulade passed on the side.

Grilled Shrimp on Arugula with Lemon Vinaigrette

Serves 4

Grilled shrimp can be great, but remember that you are dealing with shellfish that has delicate flesh. Don't overmarinate the shrimp and certainly don't overcook them! Use a little caution, and you'll be rewarded with succulent shrimp.

Shrimp

3 tablespoons extra-virgin olive oil

2 tablespoons fresh lemon juice

2 garlic cloves, crushed

1 teaspoon chopped fresh oregano

1 teaspoon chopped fresh basil

1 teaspoon chopped fresh chives

Pinch of cayenne

Salt and freshly ground pepper

24 large shrimp, peeled and deveined,
   with tails on

4 ounces green beans, cut into 1-inch lengths

2 ears of corn, unhusked

2 tablespoons balsamic vinegar, preferably
   white balsamic

2 tablespoons extra-virgin olive oil

Salt and freshly ground pepper

6 cups arugula leaves, well rinsed and dried

1 pint grape tomatoes

1 cup (packed) fresh basil leaves, torn into
   bite-size pieces

continued on next page

Grilled Shrimp on Arugula with Lemon Vinaigrette continued

To marinate the shrimp, whisk together the oil, lemon juice, garlic, oregano, basil, chives, and cayenne in a glass or other nonreactive bowl and season to taste with salt and pepper. Pour into a zippered plastic bag and add the shrimp. Marinate in the refrigerator for 2 hours.

Bring a medium saucepan of lightly salted water to a boil over high heat. Add the green beans and cook just until crisp-tender, about 3 minutes. Drain and rinse under cold water. Pat dry with paper towels.

Build a charcoal fire in an outdoor grill or pre-heat a gas grill. Grill the corn, covered, turning often, until the husks are charred, about 20 minutes. Husk the corn and remove the silks. Cut the corn off the cobs. Cool.

If using a charcoal grill, the coals will have burned down to medium-hot. If using a gas grill, adjust the heat to medium. Lightly oil the grill grate.

Grill the shrimp, turning once, until firm and bright pink or orange, 4 to 5 minutes.

Whisk together the balsamic vinegar and olive oil. Season to taste with salt and pepper. Place the arugula, green beans, tomatoes, corn, and basil in a large bowl and toss with the vinaigrette. Divide evenly among 4 large plates and arrange the grilled shrimp next to the salad. Serve immediately.

Gulf Shrimp Stew

Makes 6 to 8 servings

This stew is loaded with the flavors of the Gulf Coast. If you have the time, simmer the shrimp shells in the chicken broth for ten minutes to make a quick shrimp broth that will add a bit of extra flavor. Measure the broth and add water if needed to make two cups.

4 strips of bacon

1 tablespoon extra-virgin olive oil

1 medium onion, chopped

3 celery ribs, chopped

3 garlic cloves, minced

2 tablespoons all-purpose flour

4 cups chopped Roma or plum tomatoes
   (about 1 1/2 pounds) or drained and
   chopped canned tomatoes

2 cups Chicken Broth (page 46) or canned
   low-sodium broth

2 pounds large shrimp, peeled and deveined

Salt and freshly ground black pepper

Chopped fresh parsley, for garnish

Cooked white rice, for serving

Cook the bacon in a 12-inch skillet over medium heat until crisp and brown, about 5 minutes. Using a slotted spatula, transfer the bacon to paper towels. Pour off all but 1 tablespoon of bacon fat from the skillet.

Add the oil to the skillet and return to medium heat. Add the onion, celery, and garlic and cook, stirring often, until the onion is translucent, about 6 minutes. Sprinkle with the flour and stir well. Add the tomatoes and broth. Crumble the reserved bacon and return to the skillet.

Bring to a boil over high heat. Reduce the heat to medium-low. Simmer, partially covered, until nicely thickened, about 25 minutes.

Stir in the shrimp and increase the heat to high. Cook, stirring often, until the shrimps are firm, 3 to 5 minutes.

Season to taste with salt and pepper. Sprinkle with parsley. Serve hot with rice.

Broiled Fish Fillets with Tomato Vinaigrette

Makes 4 servings

Once you have this tomato vinaigrette in your repertoire, you will use it again and again. It goes with salads as well as broiled fish.

Four 6-ounce firm white-fleshed fish fillets,
   such as orange roughy or snapper
1 tablespoon extra-virgin olive oil
Salt and freshly ground black pepper

Tomato Vinaigrette

1 large ripe tomato (about 10 ounces), cored,
   peeled, seeded, and chopped (see page 30)
3 tablespoons sherry vinegar (see Note)
1 garlic clove, crushed through a press
1/4 cup extra-virgin olive oil
2 tablespoons chopped fresh basil
Salt and freshly ground black pepper

Position the broiler pan 6 inches from the source of heat and preheat. Lightly oil the broiler rack.

Lightly season the fish with salt and pepper. Broil, turning once, until the fish looks opaque when pierced in the center with the tip of a knife, about 6 minutes.

Meanwhile make the vinaigrette. In a food processor or blender, pulse the tomato, vinegar, and garlic until finely chopped. With the machine running, gradually pour in the oil. Pour into a bowl and stir in the basil. Season to taste with salt and pepper.

Transfer the fish to dinner plates. Spoon some of the vinaigrette over the fish, and pass the remainder at the table.

Note: *Sherry vinegar, made from sherry and usually imported from Spain, is milder than wine vinegar. It is available at specialty grocers and by mail order (see Sources, page 278). Balsamic vinegar is an acceptable substitute.*

Grilled Fish Fillets with Watercress Mustard and Tarragon

Makes 6 servings

Laurent du Clos Watercress Mustard is a favorite ingredient of mine – it is so flavorful I am always looking for new ways to use it. Here it becomes a quick glaze for grilled fish fillets, and can be used on any fish that you care to grill. If you prefer, broil the fish on an oiled broiler rack.

1/4 cup Laurent du Clos Watercress Mustard

    (see Note)

2 tablespoons fresh lemon juice

1 tablespoon extra-virgin olive oil

1 tablespoon chopped fresh parsley

2 teaspoons chopped fresh tarragon or

    1 teaspoon dried tarragon

2 garlic cloves, crushed through a press

Six 6-ounce firm white-fleshed fish fillets,

    such as tilapia, grouper, or striped bass,

    skin removed

Salt and freshly ground black pepper

Lemon wedges, for serving

Build a charcoal fire in an outdoor grill and let it burn until the coals are covered with ashes and have burned down to medium-hot (you should be able to hold your hand above the coals at rack level for about 3 seconds). Or preheat a gas grill on High, then adjust the heat to medium.

In a blender or mini-chopper, purée the mustard, lemon juice, oil, parsley, tarragon, and garlic. Season the fish lightly with salt and pepper.

Lightly oil the grill rack. Place the fillets on the grill and brush with half of the mustard mixture.

Grill for 2 1/2 minutes. Turn the fillets, brush with the remaining mustard, and grill until the fish looks opaque when pierced with the tip of a knife, about 3 minutes more. Serve hot, with the lemon wedges.

Note: *Laurent de Clos Watercress Mustard is available at specialty food stores and by phone and by mail order (see* Sources, *page 278). If necessary, substitute 1/4 cup Dijon mustard and 2 tablespoons minced watercress leaves for the watercress mustard.*

Spicy and Crispy Catfish Fillets

Makes 8 servings

The secret to this dish is Old Bay Seasoning, a terrific blend of spices that you'll find in many supermarkets and fish stores. And be sure your oven is preheated well so the fish crisps up nicely. I love these with Indiana Spoon Bread (page 155) and Homemade Ketchup (page 30).

Nonstick cooking oil spray

Eight 5- to 6-ounce catfish fillets

1 tablespoon Old Bay Seasoning or other

    spice blend for fish

1/2 cup buttermilk

1 large egg

1 cup seasoned dried breadcrumbs

Position a rack in the top third of the oven and preheat to 400°F. Spray a large baking sheet with cooking spray.

continued on next page

Spicy and Crispy Catfish Fillets continued

Season the fish all over with the seasoning. In a shallow dish, whisk the buttermilk and egg to combine. Dip the fillets in the buttermilk, then coat on both sides with the breadcrumbs. Arrange in a single layer on the baking sheet. Spray the fillets with the oil.

Bake for 8 minutes. Carefully turn the fillets and spray again with oil. Bake until crispy, about 8 minutes more. Serve hot.

Baked Cod with Thyme-Walnut Butter and Baby Spinach

Makes 4 servings

Cod, with its sweet, flaky flesh, is one of the most commonly available fish. So much so, it can be taken for granted by some cooks. Here, it is given the just-right treatment with a thyme-walnut butter and served on a bed of baby spinach.

Thyme-Walnut Butter

8 tablespoons (1 stick) unsalted butter,
  at room temperature

1/3 cup finely chopped walnuts

1 1/2 teaspoons chopped fresh thyme

1/4 teaspoon salt

1/8 teaspoon freshly ground black pepper

Four 6- to 8-ounce cod fillets

Salt and freshly ground black pepper

1/3 cup all-purpose flour

3 tablespoons extra-virgin olive oil

Two 10-ounce bags baby spinach

To make the walnut butter, mash the butter, walnuts, thyme, salt, and pepper in a small bowl with a rubber spatula to combine. On a piece of parchment paper, form the butter into a thick log and wrap. Refrigerate until the butter is firm, at least 1 hour. (The walnut butter can be prepared up to 1 week ahead and refrigerated, or frozen, overwrapped in aluminum foil, for up to 2 months.)

Position a rack in the center of the oven and preheat to 350°F.

Season the fish with salt and pepper. Place the flour in a shallow dish. Coat the fish in the flour, shaking off the excess. Heat 2 tablespoons of the oil in a large ovenproof skillet over medium-high heat. Add the fish and cook, turning once, until golden on both sides, about 4 minutes.

Slice the walnut butter into 8 equal pats. Place 2 pats on each cod fillet. Bake until the cod is opaque when flaked with the tip of a knife, about 10 minutes.

Meanwhile, in another large skillet, heat the remaining 1 tablespoon oil over medium-high heat. In batches, add the spinach, stirring until each batch wilts before adding more. Cook until tender, about 5 minutes. Season to taste with salt and pepper.

Divide the spinach among 4 dinner plates. Place a cod fillet on top of each bed of spinach. Serve immediately.

Seared Tuna Niçoise Salad with Lemon Vinaigrette

Makes 4 servings

Tuna is a fish that you just can't serve well done – once it goes over the medium-rare stage, it dries out. Searing a large tuna "roast" in a skillet will give you the proper rare-in-the-center result. Combined with the vegetables found in a niçoise salad, this tuna makes a wonderful meal for a warm evening.

Lemon Vinaigrette

1/4 cup fresh lemon juice

2 teaspoons minced shallot

1 teaspoon minced fresh thyme

1 cup extra-virgin olive oil

Salt and freshly ground black pepper

5 ounces green beans, trimmed

1 1/2 pounds small new potatoes, scrubbed
  but not peeled

One 1 1/4-pound piece of center-cut tuna,
  skin removed

Salt and freshly ground black pepper

2 heads Bibb lettuce, separated into
  individual leaves

1/2 pint red or yellow tiny pear tomatoes

1 cup pitted and coarsely chopped black
  Mediterranean olives, such as kalamata

To make the vinaigrette, whisk the lemon juice, shallot, and thyme in a small bowl. Gradually whisk in the oil to make a thick dressing. Season to taste with salt and pepper.

Bring a medium saucepan of lightly salted water to a boil over high heat. Add the green beans and cook until crisp-tender, about 3 minutes. Drain, rinse under cold water, pat dry with paper towels, and cool.

Place the potatoes in a large saucepan, cover with lightly salted water, and bring to a boil over high heat. Reduce the heat to medium and cook until the potatoes are tender when pierced with the tip of a knife, about 15 minutes. Drain, rinse under cold water, and cool. Slice into 1/8-inch rounds and cool.

Heat a large nonstick skillet over medium-high heat. Season the tuna with salt and pepper. Cook, turning occasionally, until the tuna is seared and light brown on all sides (don't bother to sear the ends of the tuna), about 10 minutes. The tuna should be rare in the center. Transfer to a plate. Cool completely. If desired, cover and refrigerate until serving.

To serve, arrange the lettuce in a decorative bed on a large platter. Cut the tuna crosswise into 1/4-inch slices. Overlap the slices at one end of the platter. Toss the potatoes with 2 tablespoons of the dressing and mound at another end of the platter. Toss the green beans with another 2 tablespoons of the dressing and lean up against the potatoes to give the dish some height. Scatter the olives and tomatoes over the salad. Drizzle with a few tablespoons of the dressing.

Serve immediately, with the remaining dressing on the side.

It energizes me to fulfill special requests from family members; I know how pleased they will be when they see their heart's desire appear on the dinner table.

Wherever we are in this world, at the end of the day we come home to our personal sanctuary for

dinner. Without doubt, everyone can relate to the end-of-the-day quandary about what to eat.

Italian Vegetable Casserole

Makes 6 servings

Grilling the vegetables before baking gives them a subtle smokiness that makes this casserole special. For extraordinary results, use fresh mozzarella (the kind stored in water at Italian delicatessens and cheese shops).

4 tablespoons extra-virgin olive oil

1 medium onion, chopped

2 garlic cloves, finely chopped

One 15-ounce can crushed tomatoes

1/4 cup chopped fresh basil

Salt and freshly ground black pepper

1 medium eggplant, peeled and cut lengthwise
    into 3/4-inch-thick slices

3 medium zucchini, scrubbed and cut length-
    wise into 1/2-inch-thick slices

2 medium red bell peppers, tops and bottoms
    trimmed and reserved, flesh opened into
    1 long strip, ribs and seeds removed

8 ounces mozzarella cheese, preferably fresh,
    thinly sliced

1/3 cup dried breadcrumbs

1/3 cup freshly grated Parmesan cheese

Heat 2 tablespoons of the oil in a large skillet over medium heat. Add the onion and cook until translucent, about 5 minutes. Add the garlic and stir until fragrant, about 1 minute. Stir in the tomatoes and bring to a simmer. Reduce the heat to low and simmer until thickened, about 10 minutes. Stir in the basil and season to taste with salt and pepper. Set aside.

Build a charcoal fire in an outdoor grill and let it burn until the coals are covered with white ashes. For a gas grill, preheat on High. Lightly oil the grill grate.

Brush the sliced eggplant and zucchini with the remaining 2 tablespoons of oil (or spray with olive oil in a mister). Place on the grill, and add the red pepper strips, tops, and bottoms, skin side down. Cover and grill, and removing each vegetable from the grill as it is cooked. Grill the eggplant and zucchini, turning once, until tender, about 8 minutes. Season to taste with salt and pepper. Grill the peppers until the skin is charred and blistered, about 10 minutes. Cool, then peel. Season to taste with salt and pepper.

Position a rack in the center of the oven and preheat to 350°F. Lightly oil a 2-quart shallow baking dish.

Spread a thin layer of the tomato sauce in the bottom of the dish. Layer the vegetables (in any order), mozzarella, and remaining tomato sauce in the dish, ending with a layer of vegetables. Mix the breadcrumbs and Parmesan in a small bowl and sprinkle on top.

Bake until the juices are bubbling and the top is golden brown, about 30 minutes. Let stand for 5 minutes before serving.

Stuffed Eggplant and Roasted Tomato Sauce

Makes 6 servings

A simple stuffed eggplant gets the star treatment when served with roasted tomato sauce. If you wish, add four ounces of finely chopped prosciutto to the stuffing.

6 medium globe eggplants, tops trimmed,
   cut in half lengthwise

4 tablespoons extra-virgin olive oil

Salt and freshly ground black pepper

1 medium onion, chopped

2 celery ribs, chopped

1 medium red bell pepper, seeded and chopped

2 garlic cloves, minced

2 ripe Roma or plum tomatoes, seeded
   and chopped

1 tablespoon tomato paste dissolved in
   $^1/_4$ cup water

2 teaspoons chopped fresh thyme or 1 teaspoon
   dried thyme

1 cup (4 ounces) chopped mozzarella cheese

$^1/_2$ cup fresh breadcrumbs

$^1/_2$ cup freshly grated Parmesan cheese

Roasted Tomato Sauce (page 34), for serving

Position a rack in the center of the oven and preheat to 350°F. Lightly oil a shallow baking dish.

Make crosshatches in the cut surface of each eggplant half with a sharp paring knife, coming within $^1/_2$ inch of the bottom and sides. Scoop out the insides of eggplant halves, leaving a $^1/_2$-inch-thick shell. Brush the inside of the eggplant shells with 1 tablespoon of the oil and season to taste with salt and pepper. Coarsely chop the eggplant flesh.

Heat 2 tablespoons of the oil in a large skillet over medium heat. Add the onion, celery, and bell pepper. Cook, stirring often, until softened, about 3 minutes. Add the chopped eggplant and garlic, and cook, stirring, until the eggplant softens, about 5 minutes. Stir in the tomatoes, dissolved tomato paste, and thyme and cook until the tomatoes are heated through, about 2 minutes. Pour into a large bowl and stir in the mozzarella and breadcrumbs. Season to taste with salt and pepper.

Spoon the filling into the shells. Drizzle with the remaining 1 tablespoon oil. Bake for 30 minutes, then sprinkle with the Parmesan cheese. Bake until the eggplant shells are tender when pierced with a knife, about 15 minutes. Serve hot, with the tomato sauce.

Potatoes in Tomato Sauce

Makes 4 servings

Serve this luxuriously spiced Pakistani dish with Naan (page 71) or even flour tortillas for a filling vegetarian main course.

3 tablespoons vegetable oil

2 jalapeño chiles, seeded and finely diced

1 teaspoon cumin seeds

1/2 teaspoon fennel seeds

1/2 teaspoon black onion seeds
  (see *Sources*, page 278)

1/2 teaspoon black mustard seeds (see *Sources*,
  page 278)

4 medium Yukon Gold potatoes, peeled and cut
  into 1/2-inch cubes (about 1 1/2 pounds)

3 large tomatoes, diced

2 teaspoons tomato paste

1/4 teaspoon cayenne

Salt

2 1/2 cups water

1/2 cup chopped fresh cilantro

Juice of 1 lime

Heat the oil in a large skillet over medium-high heat. Add the jalapeños, cumin seeds, fennel seeds, black onion seeds, and black mustard seeds and stir until the seeds begin to pop.

Add the potatoes and cook until they begin to soften, about 5 minutes. Stir in the tomatoes, tomato paste, cayenne, and salt to taste and cook until the tomatoes begin to give off their juices, about 5 minutes. Add the water and bring to a boil over medium-high heat. Reduce the heat to medium-low and cover. Simmer until the potatoes are tender and the sauce has thickened, 15 to 20 minutes.

Just before serving, stir in the cilantro and lime juice. Serve hot.

Fettuccine with Roasted Asparagus and Mushrooms

Makes 4 to 6 servings

Cooks looking for quick recipes should put this on their list. The ingredients for the sauce will be ready by the time the cooking water boils and the pasta is cooked.

1 pound thin asparagus, woody stems trimmed

10 ounces cremini or white button mushrooms, quartered

2 tablespoons extra-virgin olive oil

Salt and freshly ground black pepper

12 ounces egg fettuccine

4 tablespoons (1/2 stick) unsalted butter

1 small shallot, chopped

1 garlic clove, minced

1 cup ricotta cheese

1/3 cup freshly grated Parmesan cheese, plus more for serving

2 tablespoons chopped fresh chives

Position a rack in the top third of the oven and preheat to 450°F. Bring a large pot of lightly salted water to a boil over high heat.

Toss the asparagus and mushrooms with the oil, season to taste with salt and pepper, and spread on a large baking sheet. Bake, stirring occasionally, until just tender, 12 to 15 minutes. Cut the asparagus into 1-inch lengths. Cover loosely with aluminum foil to keep warm.

Meanwhile, cook the fettuccine in the water until barely tender.

While the pasta is cooking, heat the butter in a medium skillet over medium heat. Add the shallot and garlic and cook, stirring often, until softened, about 2 minutes.

Scoop 1/2 cup of the cooking water out of the pot and reserve. Drain the pasta and return to the pot. Add the asparagus and mushrooms, ricotta and Parmesan cheeses, garlic and shallots with their butter, and the chives. Toss, gradually adding enough of the cooking water to make a creamy sauce. Season to taste with salt and pepper. Serve hot, with additional Parmesan cheese passed on the side.

Spaghettini with Olive-Pine Nut Tomato Sauce

Makes 4 to 6 servings

Here's a pasta sauce with bold flavors, one that is quick to make from pantry ingredients. If you don't have fresh herbs, add one teaspoon each of dried basil and dried oregano to the sauce.

1/4 cup pine nuts

1/4 cup extra-virgin olive oil

4 garlic cloves, minced

1/2 teaspoon crushed red pepper

One 28-ounce can crushed tomatoes

1 cup pitted and coarsely chopped black Mediterranean-style olives, such as kalamata

1 pound spaghettini

1/4 cup chopped fresh basil

Freshly grated Parmesan cheese, for serving

Bring a large pot of lightly salted water to a boil.

Meanwhile, heat an empty large skillet over medium heat. Add the pine nuts and cook, stirring occasionally, until lightly browned, 3 to 5 minutes. Turn out onto a plate and cool.

Combine the oil, garlic, and red pepper in the skillet and heat over medium heat until the garlic is very fragrant, but not browned, about 2 minutes. Stir in the crushed tomatoes and bring to a simmer. Reduce the heat to medium-low and simmer until slightly thickened, about 15 minutes. Add the olives and cook until heated through, about 3 minutes. Keep the sauce warm.

Put the spaghettini in the boiling water and cook, stirring often, until al dente. Drain well.

Return the pasta to the pot. Add the tomato sauce, basil, and pine nuts and toss well. Serve immediately, with the cheese passed on the side.

Red Beans and Brown Rice

Makes 6 to 8 servings

A healthful vegetarian version of the Creole classic, this recipe calls for canned beans so you can have dinner on the table without thinking about presoaking dried beans. Organic canned beans have great flavor and texture.

2 cups brown rice

4 1/2 cups water

Salt

2 tablespoons extra-virgin olive oil

1 large Vidalia onion, chopped

1 small red bell pepper, seeded and chopped

1 small green bell pepper, seeded and chopped

2 garlic cloves, finely chopped

2 teaspoons salt-free Cajun seasoning

1 teaspoon ground cumin

Four 15-ounce cans small red beans, preferably organic, drained and rinsed

3 cups Vegetable Broth (page 46) or canned low-sodium broth

1 sprig of fresh thyme or 1/8 teaspoon dried thyme

1 bay leaf

1/4 cup chopped fresh parsley

Freshly ground black pepper

Hot red pepper sauce

Bring the rice, water, and 1 teaspoon of salt to a boil in a medium saucepan over high heat. Cover tightly and reduce the heat to low. Cook until the rice is tender, about 1 hour. Remove from the heat. (The rice will stay warm, tightly covered, for up to 30 minutes.)

Heat the oil in a large saucepan over medium heat. Add the onion and bell peppers. Cook, stirring occasionally, until softened, about 5 minutes. Add the garlic, Cajun seasoning, and cumin and stir for 1 minute.

Stir in the beans, broth, thyme, and bay leaf. Bring to a simmer. Cook, uncovered, stirring often, until the broth reduces slightly, 15 to 20 minutes. Stir in the parsley and season to taste with salt, pepper, and hot sauce.

Spoon the rice into bowls and top with the beans. Serve hot.

Scalloped Potatoes with Sun-Dried Tomato Pesto

Makes 8 servings

These scalloped potatoes are made with broth, not milk, and get extra flavor from sun-dried tomato pesto. They are fabulous with roast chicken.

3 pounds Yukon Gold potatoes

1 cup Sun-Dried Tomato Pesto (page 28)

Salt and freshly ground black pepper

2 cups (8 ounces) shredded sharp
   Cheddar cheese

2 tablespoons chopped fresh basil or 1 tablespoon chopped fresh marjoram

1 cup Chicken Broth (page 46) or canned
   low-sodium broth, heated to boiling

2 tablespoons chopped fresh parsley

Position a rack in the center of the oven and preheat to 400°F. Lightly oil an 11 1/2 x 8-inch (2-quart) baking dish. Bring a large pot of lightly salted water to a boil over high heat.

Peel the potatoes and cut into 1/8-inch-thick rounds (a mandoline or food processor does the quickest work). Add to the boiling water and cook until barely tender, about 8 minutes. Drain and toss with the pesto to coat evenly. Season to taste with salt and pepper.

Layer half of the potatoes in the dish, sprinkle with one third of the cheese, and sprinkle with basil. Continue until you have 3 layers, finishing with cheese. Pour in the hot broth. Cover tightly with aluminum foil.

Bake for 30 minutes. Uncover and continue to bake until the cheese is bubbling and starting to brown, about 15 minutes. Serve hot, sprinkled with parsley.

Grilled Zucchini with Balsamic Vinegar and Mint

Makes 4 to 6 servings

One of the easiest side dishes, and one of the best.

1/4 cup extra-virgin olive oil

3 garlic cloves, finely chopped

4 medium zucchini, scrubbed and cut in half
   lengthwise

Salt and freshly ground black pepper

2 tablespoons balsamic vinegar

1/3 cup coarsely chopped mint

Heat the oil and garlic in a small saucepan over low heat, just until the garlic is very aromatic, about 2 minutes. Remove from the heat.

Build a charcoal fire in an outdoor grill and let it burn until the coals are covered with white ashes. In a gas grill, preheat on High.

Brush the zucchini with some of the garlic oil and season to taste with salt and pepper. Grill the zucchini, skin side down, until it begins to soften, about 3 minutes. Turn and cook until tender, 3 to 6 minutes more, depending on the size of the zucchini.

Cut each zucchini half at a sharp angle into 2 or 3 pieces and place in a bowl. Add the vinegar, mint, and the remaining garlic oil. Toss well. Season with additional salt and pepper. Serve warm or cool to room temperature.

Fava Beans with Pecorino Curls

Makes 4 to 6 servings

Fava beans are beloved by Mediterranean cooks, and our American chefs have taken them to heart too. The beans have a fresh flavor that says spring. They must be removed from their thick velvet-like pods, then peeled, so you may want to get a friend to help out.

3 pounds fresh fava beans, shelled (about
   3 1/2 cups shelled beans)

1/3 cup extra-virgin olive oil

2 garlic cloves, finely chopped

1/2 teaspoon crushed red pepper

Salt and freshly ground black pepper

Large chunk of Tuscan Pecorino cheese,
   for the curls

Bring a large pot of lightly salted water to a boil. Add the beans and cook just until the skins loosen, about 1 minute. Drain and rinse under cold water. Peel the beans.

Heat the oil, garlic, and red pepper in a medium skillet over medium-high heat until the garlic is softened but not browned, about 2 minutes. Add the beans and toss until heated through and coated with the oil, about 1 minute. Season to taste with salt and pepper.

Transfer to a serving bowl. Using a vegetable peeler, shave curls of the Pecorino cheese over the beans. Serve immediately.

Broccoli Rabe with Sweet Chile Sauce

Makes 4 to 6 servings

Broccoli rabe (also called rapini) has a pleasant bitterness that seems to go especially well with pork dishes. It tastes nothing like broccoli, but it does look a little like broccoli florets. If you're considering a side dish for the Asian Barbecued Ribs (page 134), give this a try.

3 bunches (2¾ pounds) broccoli rabe, trimmed

3 tablespoons extra-virgin olive oil

4 cloves garlic, sliced paper thin

¼ cup Thai or Chinese sweet chile sauce
   (see *Sources*, page 278)

Salt

Bring a large pot of lightly salted water to a boil. Cook the broccoli rabe just until tender, about 3 minutes. Drain and rinse under cool water.

Heat the olive oil and garlic in a large skillet over medium heat until the garlic is soft and light gold, about 3 minutes. Add the broccoli rabe and cook, stirring often, until heated through, about 3 minutes. Toss with the sweet chile sauce and season with salt. Serve immediately.

Mashed Potato Casserole

Makes 10 to 12 servings

It's Sunday supper for lots of friends and family, and you want to serve mashed potatoes but without the last-minute hassle. Here's the recipe I use when I'm in that spot; some folks like these mashed potatoes better than the old-fashioned kind.

4 pounds Yukon Gold potatoes, peeled and
   cut into ¾-inch chunks

8 ounces light cream cheese, cut into pieces,
   at room temperature

1 cup (4 ounces) shredded sharp
   Cheddar cheese

⅔ cup milk

2 tablespoons unsalted butter

Salt and freshly ground pepper

2 tablespoons chopped fresh chives

Position a rack in the center of the oven and preheat to 350°F. Butter a 13 x 9-inch baking dish.

Place the potatoes in a large saucepan and add enough lightly salted water to cover by 1 inch. Bring to a boil over high heat. Reduce the heat to medium-low. Simmer until the potatoes are tender, about 15 minutes. Drain and return to the pot.

Mash the potatoes until chunky with a hand-held electric mixer. Add the cream cheese, ¾ cup of the Cheddar, milk, butter, and salt and pepper to taste and mix until smooth. Stir in the chives. Spread evenly in the baking dish and top with remaining ¾ cup of Cheddar.

Bake until the cheese is melted and the casserole is heated through, about 30 minutes. Serve hot. (The casserole can be prepared, without the cheese topping, up to 1 day ahead, covered, and refrigerated. If chilled, add the cheese topping and bake until heated through, about 45 minutes.)

Basmati Rice and Peas

Makes 6 servings

Fragrant basmati rice stands up to the aromatic spices that make this dish so popular with Pakistani cooks. Be sure to warn your guests not to bite into the spices when they eat the rice!

1 teaspoon finely chopped garlic

1 teaspoon peeled and finely chopped fresh ginger

1 teaspoon salt

3 tablespoons vegetable oil

6 whole cloves

2 whole black cardamom (see Note)

1 large cinnamon stick, broken into 3 pieces

1/2 teaspoon cumin seeds

1/2 teaspoon black cumin seeds or additional cumin seeds (see Note)

1/2 cup finely chopped onion

4 whole dried red chiles

2 cups basmati rice

1 1/2 cups fresh or defrosted frozen peas

4 cups water, as needed

Chop and mash the garlic, ginger, and salt into a paste. Scrape into a small bowl.

Heat the oil in a heavy-bottomed, medium saucepan over medium heat. Add the cloves, cardamom, cinnamon, cumin, and black cumin and stir until fragrant, about 1 1/2 minutes. Add the onion and cook, stirring occasionally, until translucent, about 3 minutes. Stir in the garlic-ginger paste and chiles and stir for 1 minute more. Add the rice and fresh peas (if using thawed peas, add them later) and stir until the rice turns from translucent to opaque, about 2 minutes.

Add enough water to cover the rice by 1 inch (about 4 cups). Bring to a boil over high heat. Reduce the heat to low and cover tightly. Cook until all the liquid has been absorbed, about 20 to 25 minutes. If using thawed frozen peas, add them to the rice (do not stir) during the last 5 minutes of cooking.

Remove from the heat and let stand 5 to 10 minutes. Fluff with a fork and serve hot.

Note: *Black cardamom and black cumin seeds are available by mail order (see* Sources, *page 278).*

Roasted Vegetables with Cider Glaze

Makes 6 to 8 servings

Roasted root vegetables are delicious enough, but I've taken to adding a simple apple cider and butter glaze to give them a sweet-and-sour twist.

1/2 celery root, pared and cut into
  1-inch cubes

3 tablespoons extra-virgin olive oil

Salt and freshly ground black pepper

4 medium carrots, peeled and cut into
  1-inch lengths

2 medium onions, peeled and quartered

3 celery ribs, cut into 1-inch lengths

2 medium parsnips, cut into 1-inch lengths

1 medium turnip, peeled and cut into
  1-inch cubes

1/4 cup apple cider

1/4 cup Chicken Broth (page 46) or canned
  low-sodium broth

2 tablespoons unsalted butter

1 tablespoon maple syrup

Position 2 racks in the center and top third of the oven and preheat to 400°F. Lightly oil 2 large baking sheets.

Toss the celery root in a medium bowl with 1 tablespoon of oil and season to taste with salt and pepper. Spread on a baking sheet. Bake on the top rack for 20 minutes.

Toss the carrots, onions, celery, parsnips, and turnip with the remaining 2 tablespoons oil and season to taste with salt and pepper. Divide between the 2 baking sheets, adding to the celery root. Bake, stirring occasionally, until the vegetables are tender, about 1 hour.

Bring the cider, broth, butter, and maple syrup to a boil in a medium saucepan over high heat. Cook, uncovered, until reduced by half and syrupy, about 10 minutes. Season to taste with salt and pepper.

Transfer the vegetables to a serving bowl and toss with the sauce. Serve hot.

Indiana Spoon Bread

Spoon bread, for those of you who may not be familiar with it, is a soft corn bread that you can spoon out of the dish.

1/2 cup yellow cornmeal, preferably stoneground

1 cup boiling water

2 tablespoons unsalted butter

1/4 cup chopped sweet onion, such as Vidalia

1/4 cup chopped green or red bell pepper, preferably a combination of the two

1 jalapeño chile, seeded and finely chopped

2 garlic cloves, finely chopped

2 cups fresh corn kernels (from 4 ears)

1 small tomato, peeled, seeded, and chopped (see Note, page 30)

1/2 cup buttermilk

3 large eggs, separated, at room temperature

1 teaspoon baking powder

1 teaspoon sugar

1/4 teaspoon baking soda

1/4 teaspoon salt

1/4 cup plus 2 tablespoons freshly grated Parmesan cheese

Position a rack in the center of the oven and preheat to 375°F. Lightly butter a 13 x 9-inch baking dish.

Whisk the cornmeal and boiling water in a medium bowl. Cool slightly.

Heat 1 tablespoon of the butter in a medium skillet over medium heat. Add the onion, bell pepper, and jalapeño and cook, stirring often, until softened, about 3 minutes. Add the garlic and cook for 1 minute. Remove from the heat and stir in the corn and tomato.

Whisk the remaining 1 tablespoon butter into the cornmeal mixture. Whisk in the buttermilk. One at a time, whisk in the egg yolks, then the baking powder, sugar, baking soda, and salt. Mix in the vegetables.

Beat the egg whites in a medium bowl until stiff peaks begin to form. Stir about one fourth of the whites into the cornmeal mixture, then fold in the rest. Fold in 1/4 cup Parmesan cheese. Carefully spread in the dish and sprinkle with the remaining 2 tablespoons Parmesan cheese.

Bake until puffed and golden brown, 30 to 35 minutes.

Family Traditions

For me, family tradition is practiced daily, not just on holidays and planned family get-togethers. The key is to enjoy your loved ones every time you're together.

Family Reunions

Twice a year my family and every kissin' cousin in a 200-mile radius got together for a family reunion. These were occasions of great food and even better stories, but I confess I rarely enjoyed them as much as the smaller, more spontaneous reunions we had most weekends.

The reunions, small and large, often happened near one of the many deep water springs along the Suwannee River. We kids loved to swim in these cold, clear pools. If we were lucky, we would spot a giant, gentle Florida manatee swimming upstream from the Gulf of Mexico.

The only requirement at these reunions was to bring a dish. This might be Old-Fashioned Potato Salad, a plate of Deviled Eggs, Chicken and Biscuits, or Southern Sweet Potato Pie. The food and the flavors were as diverse as the folks who gathered along the banks of the Suwannee. But one thing was always true: Family members gave a piece of their heart with their special dishes.

Family reunions allow us to connect and reconnect with relatives. It's fun to spot your own nose or ears on someone else, to hear stories told over and over, and to laugh at the timeworn jokes. These gatherings also provide a sense of where you came from and how you became the person you are.

Two family reunions stand out among all the others for me, the first when I was still in high school and the second when I was a grown man.

Because of my red hair, I was convinced for years that I was adopted. I searched high and low for the adoption papers my mother swore did not exist. "Honey, I can just remember your little red wet head," she told me in reply to questions about my birth. As I got older, I became increasingly suspicious. I was so different from my brother. He wanted nothing more than to farm, while I wanted to go on the stage, play the piano, and draw from dawn until dusk. How could God have put me with this family? As sweet as they were, they couldn't possibly understand who I was.

At a family reunion I met my great-aunt Millicent, my grandmother's sister. What an extraordinary person she is! She asked me to play the piano for her; she told me tales of her life in New York City, where she had been involved in show business and fashion, working for a time as the fashion consultant for *The Steve Allen Show*, later to be renamed *The Tonight Show*. I was enthralled and impressed. At last I had found a kindred spirit among my relations, and we quickly became close. I traveled some with Aunt Millicent and learned that there was a larger world beyond Jasper, Florida. I think of her as my own personal Auntie Mame.

At another reunion, nearly twenty years later, I ran into a cousin named Sheron Leonard. As we took a walk down a dusty dirt road, we discovered we had much in common, particularly when she told me she was writing a play inspired by seeing the AIDS Quilt in San Francisco. This play would go on to become a musical called *In Stitches*, eventually performed during the Atlanta Olympic Games in 1996.

These two women were part of my family. I felt connected and honored to know them, and best of all, I felt I was home.

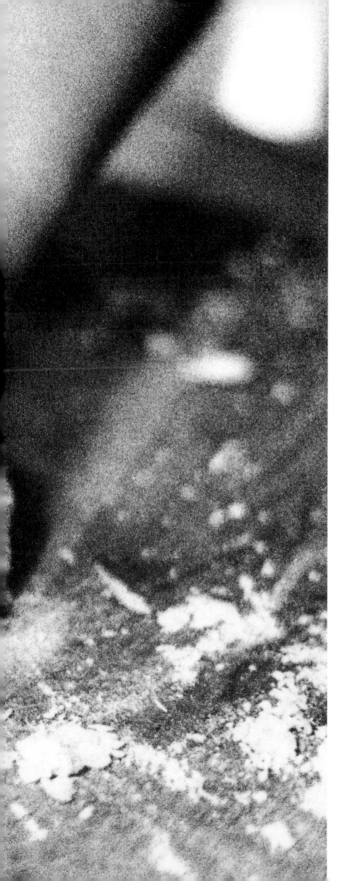

Fresh Pasta Dough

Makes about 1 pound

When I needed pasta recipes for my book, I called upon my friend Domenica Catelli, "the reigning pasta queen," who on countless occasions has created a multitude of pasta dishes at a moment's notice. For the silkiest, smoothest pasta, make it at home. The process is simple and lots of fun. While you can run the pasta through the cutting rollers of the machine, I like the rustic look of pasta cut by hand with a knife.

2 cups all-purpose flour, plus additional
   for dusting

3 large eggs, beaten

1/4 teaspoon salt

Place the flour, eggs, and salt in the bowl of a heavy-duty mixer fitted with the paddle blade. Mix on medium-low speed until the dough comes together into a ball. Switch to the dough hook and knead on medium-low speed until the dough is smooth and supple, about 10 minutes. Remove from the bowl, form into a ball, and cover with plastic wrap. Let stand at room temperature for at least 30 minutes and up to 2 hours.

Cover a large table with a tablecloth and dust lightly with flour. Cut the dough into 4 equal pieces. Work with 1 piece of dough at a time, keeping the remaining pieces covered with plastic wrap. Attach the pasta machine to the work surface. Place about 1/2 cup of flour next to the machine.

continued on next page

Fresh Pasta Dough continued

Adjust the rollers in the pasta machine to the widest setting. Dust the piece of dough on both sides with flour and crank the machine to run the dough through the rollers. Fold the dough into thirds, dust with flour, and run through the machine. Repeat the procedure 3 or 4 times, until the dough smooths out. Adjust the rollers to the next setting, and run the dough through 2 or 3 times, dusting with flour as needed. Repeat with each setting, stopping at the second-to-last setting. Place the sheet of dough on the table-cloth and let dry until the surface feels leathery but not brittle (the dough should be supple), about 10 minutes, depending on the humidity.

One at a time, as they dry, transfer the pasta sheets to the work surface. Using a pizza wheel, cut the dough by hand into the size you want, transfer to a large baking sheet, cover with plastic wrap, and refrigerate until ready to cook.

Variations

Fettuccine: Cut into 1/4-inch wide ribbons.

Fresh Lasagna Noodles: Trim off the pointed edges, and cut the pasta sheets into 13-inch lengths.

Homemade Ravioli, Three Ways

Makes 48 to 50 ravioli, 6 main-course servings or 8 appetizer servings

By using store-bought wonton wrappers instead of home-made pasta, you can whip up fresh ravioli whenever the inspiration strikes. It is difficult for me to choose a filling, so I am providing recipes for my three favorites: four-cheese, mushroom and spinach, or pumpkin and sage. Choose one filling, and serve the ravioli in a shallow portion of chicken soup as a "sauce."

Other sauce possibilities include Roasted Tomato Sauce (page 34) with the cheese or mushroom ravioli or browned butter and fresh sage for the pumpkin version.

Four-Cheese Filling

1 1/2 cups ricotta cheese

2/3 cup crumbled chèvre (soft goat cheese), at room temperature

1/2 cup freshly grated Parmesan cheese

1/4 cup crumbled blue cheese, such as Gorgonzola, at room temperature

3 tablespoons finely chopped fresh parsley

Salt and freshly ground black pepper

Mushroom-Spinach Filling

3 tablespoons extra-virgin olive oil

2 garlic cloves, finely chopped

1/4 teaspoon crushed red pepper

20 ounces assorted mushrooms, such as cremini, shiitake, or white button mushrooms, finely chopped

3 tablespoons chopped fresh parsley

1 tablespoons chopped fresh thyme or
   1 teaspoon dried thyme

Two 10-ounce bags baby spinach

Salt and freshly ground black pepper

Pumpkin and Sage Filling

2 tablespoons extra-virgin olive oil

1 medium onion, cut in half and sliced
   1/8-inch thick

2 tablespoons chopped fresh sage

One 15-ounce can solid-pack pumpkin

2/3 cup freshly grated Parmesan cheese

1/4 cup dried breadcrumbs

Salt and freshly ground black pepper

Two 12-ounce packages (50 skins each)
   wonton skins

1 large egg, beaten

1 quart Chicken Broth (page 46) or canned
   low-sodium broth

Freshly grated Parmesan cheese, for serving

To make the cheese filling, mash all of the ingredients with a rubber spatula in a medium bowl until combined.

To make the mushroom-spinach filling, heat the oil, garlic, and red pepper in a large skillet over medium heat until the garlic is softened but not browned, about 1 minute. Add the mushrooms, parsley, and thyme, and cook, stirring often, until all the liquid has evaporated and the mushrooms are tender, about 10 minutes. A handful at a time, stir in the spinach and cook until wilted

and tender. Transfer to a food processor fitted with the metal blade and purée. Season to taste with salt and pepper. Cool completely.

To make the pumpkin filling, put the oil and onion in a medium sauté pan. Cook over medium heat until the onion is soft and translucent, about 5 minutes. Add the sage and sauté for 1 minute more. Transfer to a bowl and stir in the pumpkin, cheese, and breadcrumbs. Season to taste with salt and pepper.

To make the ravioli, dust a parchment-lined baking sheet with cornstarch. Brush the perimeter of a wonton skin with the beaten egg. Place about 1 heaping teaspoon of the filling in the center, and top with another wonton skin. Press firmly to seal the edges. Place on the baking sheet. Repeat with all the skins and filling, separating the layers of ravioli with parchment. (The ravioli can be prepared up to 8 hours ahead, covered with plastic wrap, and refrigerated.)

Bring a very large pot of lightly salted water to a boil over high heat. Drop in the ravioli, stirring them occasionally to be sure they aren't sticking. Cook until the ravioli float to the surface, about 4 minutes.

Using a skimmer or wire sieve, scoop out the ravioli and divide them among soup bowls. Spoon about 1/2 cup of the hot soup into each bowl. Serve immediately, with the cheese passed on the side.

The process of making fresh pasta is simple and lots of fun.

Mix the flour, eggs, and salt.

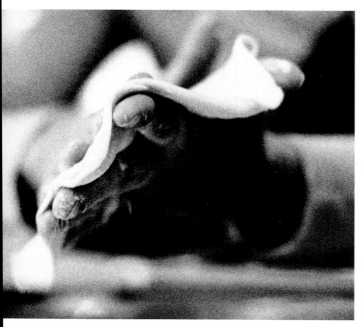

Fold the dough into thirds.

Crank the machine to roll the dough through the rollers.

Knead the dough by hand or in the bowl of a heavy-duty mixer.

Dough should be smooth and supple.

Using a pizza wheel, cut the dough by hand into the size you want.

For fettuccine, cut the dough in ¹/₄-inch-wide ribbons.

Handmade Chicken Tamales

Makes about 20 tamales

Making tamales at home is an entertaining project any time of the year, but it is during the Christmas season that most Latin families get together to stuff a corn filling into dried husks. Instead of the traditional masa harina (dried slaked corn flour) filling, I want to share a wonderful trick that works very well – cornbread batter!

24 dried corn husks (see Note)

Boiling water

2 tablespoons extra-virgin olive oil

2 pounds chicken thighs, with skin and bone

1 medium onion, chopped

4 garlic cloves, chopped

2 tablespoons chopped fresh cilantro

1 tablespoon chile powder

2 teaspoons ground cumin

1/2 teaspoon salt

1/4 teaspoon cayenne

1 cup (4 ounces) shredded Monterey Jack cheese

Batter for Classic Southern Cornbread (page 74)

Salsa Roja (page 29), for serving

Place the corn husks in a large bowl and add enough boiling water to cover. Submerge in the water by weighing down with another bowl. Let stand until the husks soften, about 1 hour. Drain well and pat dry.

Meanwhile, heat the oil in a large skillet over medium-high heat. Add the chicken and cook, turning once, until browned, about 10 minutes. Transfer to a plate.

Add the onion to the fat in the skillet and cook, stirring often, until softened, about 3 minutes.

Add the garlic and stir until fragrant, about 1 minute. Stir in the cilantro, chile powder, cumin, salt, and cayenne. Return the chicken to the skillet and add enough cold water to cover. Bring to a boil over high heat. Reduce the heat to medium-low and cover. Cook until the chicken is cooked through, about 45 minutes.

Transfer the chicken to a plate. Cool until easy to handle. Discard the skin and bones and coarsely chop the meat. Transfer to a medium bowl.

Meanwhile, let the cooking liquid stand off the heat for 5 minutes. Skim off and discard the fat on the surface. Return the skillet to the stove and bring to a boil over high heat. Cook until the liquid is reduced to a thick glaze, about 20 minutes. Scrape the glaze into the chicken, then add the cheese.

To make the tamales, place a corn husk on the work surface. Spread about 3 tablespoons of the cornbread batter in a 2- to 3-inch square area in the center of the husk. Place 1 heaping tablespoon of the chicken in the center of the batter and top with about 1 tablespoon of the batter. Fold in the sides of the husk to enclose the batter (the tamale is now about 2 1/2-inches wide). Fold over the ends of the husk so the tamale is about 3 inches long. Place the tamale, smooth side up, on the work surface. Using kitchen twine, tie up the tamale with kitchen string, gift-box fashion. Repeat with the remaining husks, batter, and chicken. (You may have some husks left over since you soaked more than you needed, in case some got torn.) Stand the tamales up, side by side, in a steamer inserted into a large pot.

continued on next page

Handmade Chicken Tamales continued

Add enough water to the pot to barely reach the bottom of the steamer. Cover tightly and bring to a boil over high heat. Reduce the heat to low. Steam the tamales until the batter is firm (open a tamale to check), about 1 hour. (The tamales can be made up to 8 hours ahead, cooled, and refrigerated. Steam over boiling water for 15 minutes to reheat.)

Serve hot, with the salsa passed on the side.

Note: *Dried corn husks are available at Latin markets and by mail order (see* Sources, *page 278).*

Cuban Paella

Makes 8 servings

This recipe has been passed down through three generations of Cuban women. Consuelo Arroyo, who leads the community chats on oprah.com, shared this with me. This recipe now continues the tradition of being passed on – from Josepha Gonzales to Georgia Gonzales, to Consuelo, to me, to you. Consuelo makes this dish once a year to remember the sacrifices that her family went through in coming to the United States and to remind her of her family's heritage.

2 tablespoons extra-virgin olive oil

One 4-pound chicken, cut into 8 serving pieces

Salt and freshly ground black pepper

8 ounces chorizo or other spicy smoked pork
   sausage, diced

2 medium onions, chopped

1 medium red bell pepper, seeded and chopped

1 medium green bell pepper, seeded
   and chopped

12 garlic cloves, finely chopped

1 cup dry white wine

4 cups Chicken Broth (page 46) or canned
   low-sodium broth

1 8-ounce can tomato sauce

1 tablespoon red wine vinegar

1 teaspoon Bejol (see Note), optional

$1/2$ teaspoon saffron

2 bay leaves

2 cups rice, preferably medium-grain

1 pound medium shrimp, peeled and deveined

2 cups defrosted frozen peas

Heat the oil in a deep 12-inch skillet over medium heat. In batches, add the chicken and cook, turning occasionally, until browned, about 10 minutes. Transfer to a plate. Season the chicken with $1/2$ teaspoon salt and $1/4$ teaspoon pepper.

Add the chorizo, onions, red and green peppers and cook, stirring occasionally, until the onions are translucent, about 10 minutes. Add the garlic and cook until fragrant, about 2 minutes. Stir in the wine and bring to a boil. Cook until slightly reduced, about 3 minutes.

Stir in the broth, tomato sauce, vinegar, Bejol (if using), saffron, and bay leaves. Bring to a boil over high heat. Cook until slightly reduced, about 10 minutes. Stir in the rice and $1/2$ teaspoon salt and bring to a boil. Cover tightly and reduce the heat to low. Cook for 15 minutes. Scatter the shrimp and peas over the rice (do not stir). Cook until the rice is tender and the shrimp are firm, about 5 minutes more.

Remove from the heat and let stand for 5 to 15 minutes (the rice will absorb any remaining liquid in the skillet). Serve hot.

Note: *Bejol, an annatto-based seasoning, is really used more for coloring food golden yellow than for flavor. It can be found at Latin markets, or you can simply leave it out.*

Tomato-Smothered Catfish

Makes 8 servings

There's more than one way to smother food. The typical method uses broth or water, but my friend, cookbook author Wilbert Jones, likes to use vegetable-studded tomato and wine sauce. Instead of white rice, you might want to serve this with orzo, the rice-shaped pasta.

4 tablespoons vegetable oil, preferably
   canola oil, as needed

Eight 7-ounce catfish fillets

1/4 cup fresh lemon juice

Salt and freshly ground black pepper

1/2 cup all-purpose flour

1 medium onion, chopped

1 medium green bell pepper, ribs and
   seeds removed, chopped

1 medium red bell pepper, ribs and seeds
   removed, chopped

2 garlic cloves, finely chopped

1 cup dry white wine

One 15-ounce can tomato sauce

1 tablespoon chopped fresh tarragon or
   1 teaspoon dried tarragon

1 teaspoon chopped fresh thyme or
   1/2 teaspoon dried thyme

Heat 2 tablespoons of the oil in a large skillet over medium-high heat. In batches, dip the fillets in the lemon juice and season to taste with salt and pepper. Coat the fillets in the flour and shake off the excess. Add to the skillet and cook, turning once, until golden on both sides, about 6 minutes. Add more oil to the skillet as needed to cook the remaining fillets. Transfer to a plate.

Heat the remaining 2 tablespoons of the oil in the skillet. Add the onion and green and red peppers and cook, stirring occasionally, until the vegetables soften, about 5 minutes. Add the garlic and stir until fragrant, about 1 minute. Add the wine and bring to a boil. Stir in the tomato sauce, tarragon, and thyme and bring to a simmer. Cook, uncovered, to blend the flavors, about 5 minutes.

Return the catfish to the skillet, baste with the sauce, and cover. Simmer until the catfish is cooked through, about 5 minutes. Season to taste with salt and pepper. Serve hot.

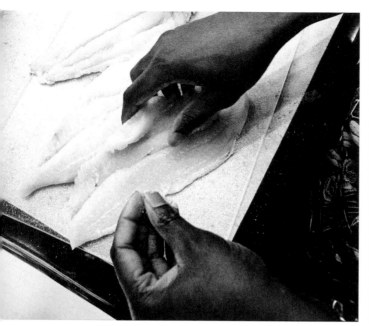

Wash and pat dry the catfish fillets.

Dip the fillets in the lemon juice and season to taste with salt and pepper.

Add more oil to the skillet as needed to cook the remaining fillets. Transfer to a plate.

Add the onion, bell peppers, and garlic and cook until the vegetables soften.

Coat the fillets in flour and shake off the excess before cooking.

Heat the oil, add the fish to the skillet, and cook, turning once, until golden on both sides.

Add the wine. Stir in the tomato sauce and herbs. Return the catfish to the skillet.

Simmer, uncovered, about 5 minutes until cooked through. Serve hot.

Butternut Squash and Sage Risotto

Makes 6 servings

There are two ways to make risotto: the time-honored, hand-stirred way or with a pressure cooker. For years my friend Ann Bloomstrand has cooked many meals for me. The most memorable is her risotto. She was the first one to teach me that you can make risotto in a pressure cooker. Try her quick method and have dinner on the table in no time.

1 small (1³⁄4 pounds) butternut squash, peeled, seeded, and cut into 1-inch cubes

2 tablespoons extra-virgin olive oil

Salt and freshly ground black pepper

6 cups Chicken Broth (page 46) or canned low-sodium broth, as needed

2 tablespoons unsalted butter

¹⁄3 cup chopped shallots

1 garlic clove, finely chopped

2 cups rice for risotto, such as Arborioa

1 cup dry white wine, such as Pinot Grigio

¹⁄2 cup freshly grated Parmesan cheese, plus more for serving

2 tablespoons chopped fresh sage

Position a rack in the top third of the oven and preheat to 400°F.

Spread the squash on a baking sheet and toss with 1 tablespoon of the oil. Season lightly with salt and pepper. Bake until tender, about 35 minutes. Remove from the oven and cover with aluminum foil to keep warm.

Bring the broth to a boil in a medium saucepan over high heat. Turn off the heat but leave the saucepan on the stove.

Melt the butter and the remaining 1 tablespoon oil in a heavy-bottomed Dutch oven or flame-proof casserole. Add the shallots and garlic and cook until softened, about 2 minutes. Add the rice and cook, stirring often, until it turns from translucent to opaque (do not brown), about 2 minutes. Add the wine and cook until almost evaporated, about 2 minutes.

Stir the hot broth into the rice, 1 cup at a time. Cook, stirring almost constantly, until the rice absorbs almost all of the broth, about 3 minutes. Stir in another cup of broth, and stir until it is almost absorbed. Repeat, keeping the risotto at a steady simmer and adding more broth as it is absorbed, until you use all of the broth and the rice is barely tender, about 20 minutes total. If you run out of broth and the rice isn't tender, use hot water. Add the squash and cook until heated through, about 1 minute. Remove from the heat and stir in the cheese. Season to taste with salt and pepper.

Serve immediately, spooned into bowls and sprinkled with the sage. Pass a bowl of Parmesan cheese on the side.

Variation

Pressure-Cooker Butternut Squash and Sage Risotto: Roast the butternut squash as directed. In a 5- to 7-quart pressure cooker or a 3-quart shallow pressure cooker (sometimes called a risotto cooker), heat the butter and remaining 1 tablespoon of oil over medium heat. Add the shallots and garlic and cook until softened, about 2 minutes. Add the rice and stir until it turns opaque, about 2 minutes. Add the unheated broth and the wine. Lock the lid in place and bring to high pressure over high heat. Adjust the heat to maintain high pressure. Cook for 7 minutes. Release the pressure according to the manufacturer's instructions or place the pot under cold water. Carefully open the lid, being careful of the steam. Stir in the cheese and season with salt and pepper. Serve immediately, sprinkled with the sage.

Matzo Ball Soup

Makes 12 to 14 servings

My adopted Jewish mother, Diane Silverman, shared her recipe for matzo ball soup. Diane says that the secret to light matzo balls is a long, gentle cooking time. You can simmer the balls right in the chicken soup. To make rendered chicken fat for the balls, pull the yellow fat from the bird and render it in a pan on top of the stove with 1 tablespoon of chopped onion and 3 tablespoons of water.

Chicken Soup

5 quarts water

One 3-4 pound hen (stewing chicken)

2 large onions, peeled and quartered

8 ribs of celery, cleaned and cut into
  $1/2$-inch sticks

8 carrots, peeled and cut into $1/2$-inch sticks

5 teaspoons of salt

Matzo Balls

6 large eggs, separated

3 tablespoons rendered chicken fat

$1^1/2$ teaspoons salt

$1^1/2$ cups matzo meal

To make the soup, place the chicken in the pot with the water. Bring to a boil and skim off the foam. Lower the heat to simmer. In order to get a clear broth you must constantly skim and never bring it past a simmer. Cook the chicken for one hour or until tender. Add the celery, carrots, and salt. Cook for 15 minutes or until the vegetables are tender. Remove the chicken from the broth and reserve for another use.

To make the matzo balls, whisk together the egg yolks, chicken fat, and salt in a large bowl. Gradually whisk in the matzo meal. The mixture will be thick, so you will have to shake it out of the whisk wires.

Beat the egg whites in a large bowl just until stiff peaks form. Stir $1/4$ of the whites into the matzo mixture to lighten, then fold in the rest. Cover the bowl with plastic wrap and refrigerate until the mixture congeals, about 1 hour.

Return the soup to a gentle boil over high heat. With wet hands, form the matzo mixture into 12 to 14 balls, dropping the balls into the simmering soup as they are formed. Cook, uncovered, until the matzo balls are cooked through, 1 to $1^1/2$ hours. Spoon the soup and matzo balls into large soup bowls and serve immediately.

My grandfather had a large garden that produced the amazing assortment of fresh fruits and

vegetables that appeared on the table. It was like having a farmers' market in the backyard.

Buttermilk Fried Chicken

Makes 4 servings

This is a great recipe from my childhood, created by Leila Curry. Use a small chicken because a larger bird just won't fit into the average skillet. Do not crowd the chicken, as this creates too much steam and prevents a crisp crust. It's best to fry the chicken in two batches, starting with the dark meat.

One 3 1/2-pound chicken, cut into 8 pieces

2 cups buttermilk

1 teaspoon salt

Vegetable oil, for frying

1 cup self-rising flour

1/2 teaspoon sweet paprika

1/4 teaspoon freshly ground black pepper

1/4 teaspoon garlic powder

Place the chicken in a medium bowl and add the buttermilk and salt. Stir well, and refrigerate for 1 hour.

Add enough oil to a deep large skillet to create a depth of 1 inch. Heat over medium-high heat to 360°F (use a deep-frying thermometer or an electric frying pan).

Mix the flour, paprika, pepper, and garlic powder in a shallow bowl. Remove the dark meat from the buttermilk, shake to remove the excess, and roll in the flour to coat. Shake off the excess flour and place in the hot oil. Cook over medium-high heat, turning occasionally, until golden brown and cooked through, about 15 minutes. Adjust the heat as needed so that the oil bubbles steadily around the chicken – it shouldn't brown too quickly. Drain on paper towels.

Reheat the oil to 360°F. Repeat with the breasts and wings, cooking for about 15 minutes.

Serve the chicken hot or at room temperature, within 2 hours of cooking.

Deviled Eggs

Makes 24 deviled eggs

Wherever people bring something to eat to a gathering, you can be sure there will be a plate of deviled eggs. Here's a classic recipe.

12 large eggs

3 tablespoons mayonnaise

2 tablespoons Dijon mustard

1 tablespoon minced sweet pickle

Dash of Worcestershire sauce

Salt and freshly ground black pepper

Hot red pepper sauce

2 tablespoons chopped fresh parsley, for garnish

Paprika, for garnish

Place the eggs in a large saucepan just large enough to hold them in a single layer. Add enough cold water to cover by 1 inch. Bring to a boil over high heat. Reduce the heat to low and simmer for 10 minutes. Drain carefully and rinse under cold water. When cool enough to handle, but still warm, peel the eggs. Cool completely.

Cut each egg in half lengthwise. Remove the yolks and place in a medium bowl. Add the mayonnaise, mustard, pickle, and Worcestershire sauce. Season to taste with salt, pepper, and hot sauce.

Transfer the yolk mixture to a pastry bag with a $1/2$-inch-wide opening. (If you wish, fit the bag with a $1/2$-inch star tip before filling.) Squeeze the yolk mixture into the hollows in the whites, and place on a serving platter. Sprinkle the filling with the parsley, and then the paprika. Cover with plastic wrap and refrigerate until chilled, at least 1 hour and up to 8 hours. Serve chilled.

Chicken in Red Wine Sauce

Makes 4 servings

This is my version of the French classic coq au vin, *with a rich sauce that is perfect for serving with noodles or steamed new potatoes. Use a full-bodied wine, such as Zinfandel or Cabernet Sauvignon.*

Marinade

3 cups hearty dry red wine, such as Zinfandel

1 small onion, chopped

1 medium carrot, chopped

1 celery rib, chopped

2 garlic cloves, sliced

1 tablespoon red wine vinegar

3 sprigs of fresh thyme or $1/2$ teaspoon
   dried thyme

2 bay leaves

One $31/2$-pound chicken, cut into quarters

Salt and freshly ground black pepper

$1/3$ cup all-purpose flour

4 tablespoons olive oil

10 ounces button mushrooms, sliced

2 tablespoons unsalted butter, cut up

To make the marinade, mix the ingredients in a nonreactive bowl.

Add the chicken and cover. Refrigerate for at least 2 hours or overnight.

Remove the chicken from the marinade and pat dry with paper towels; reserve the marinade. Season the chicken with salt and pepper. Place the flour in a shallow bowl and roll the chicken in the flour to coat, shaking off the excess flour.

Heat 2 tablespoons of the oil in a large skillet over medium-high heat. Add the chicken and cook, turning occasionally, until browned on all sides, about 7 minutes. Transfer to a plate.

Pour the marinade into the skillet and bring to a boil, scraping up any bits on the bottom of the skillet. Return the chicken to the skillet. Cover and reduce the heat to low. Simmer, turning the chicken once, until the chicken shows no sign of pink when pierced at the thigh bone, about 30 minutes. Transfer the chicken to a platter and cover with aluminum foil to keep warm.

Meanwhile, heat the remaining 2 tablespoons of oil in a separate large skillet and cook the mushrooms until browned, about 8 minutes.

Increase the heat to high under the chicken skillet and boil the sauce until thickened, about 5 minutes. Season to taste with salt and pepper. Strain into a bowl. Whisk in the butter. Spoon the mushrooms over the chicken and pour the sauce over the top. Serve hot.

Roast Chicken with Fresh Herbs

Makes 4 servings

There's no greater satisfaction than cooking a perfectly roasted chicken. Here's a recipe that ensures a crisp golden skin and a light, flavorful sauce.

One 4-pound chicken

2 garlic cloves

1 teaspoon salt

2 tablespoons extra-virgin olive oil

1 tablespoon chopped fresh tarragon

1 tablespoon chopped fresh basil

1 tablespoon chopped fresh thyme

1 tablespoon chopped fresh marjoram

1 tablespoon chopped fresh oregano

$1/2$ teaspoon freshly ground black pepper

$1/2$ lemon

1 medium onion, chopped

1 medium carrot, chopped

1 celery rib, chopped

1 cup Chicken Broth (page 46) or canned
  low-sodium broth

Position a rack in the center of the oven and preheat to 400°F.

Rinse the chicken inside and out with cold water and pat dry.

Chop and mash the garlic on a work surface with the salt to make a paste. Scrape into a small bowl. Add the oil, tarragon, basil, thyme, marjoram, oregano, and pepper. Slip your fingers under the chicken skin to loosen it as much as possible in the breast and thigh areas. Rub as much of the herb paste as you can under the skin. Rub the remaining herb paste in the body cavity, then place the lemon-half in the cavity. If desired, truss the chicken with kitchen twine.

Place the chicken, breast side up, on a rack in a roasting pan. Roast for 45 minutes. Scatter the onion, carrot, and celery in the pan. Roast until a meat thermometer inserted in the thickest part of the thigh, without touching a bone, reads 180°F.

Transfer the chicken to a platter. Discard the vegetables in the roasting pan. Pour the pan juices into a glass measuring cup. Let stand 5 minutes, then skim off any fat on the surface. Place the pan over high heat on top of the stove. When the pan is sizzling, pour in the degreased juices, then the broth. Bring to a boil, stirring up the browned bits on the bottom of the pan with a wooden spoon. Pour into a sauceboat. Carve the chicken and serve with the pan juices.

Cranberry and Pear Chutney

Makes about 3 1/2 cups

This is the perfect match to a roast turkey and dressing.

1 large navel orange

One 12-ounce bag fresh or frozen cranberries

2 Bosc pears, peeled, cored, and cut into
   1/2-inch cubes

1/4 cup chopped crystallized ginger

1/4 cup sugar

One 3-inch cinnamon stick

1/4 cup sliced almonds, toasted (see Note)

Grate the zest from the orange and squeeze
the juice.

Bring the cranberries, pears, orange juice and
zest, ginger, sugar, and cinnamon to a boil over
medium-high heat, stirring often. Reduce the
heat to medium-low. Simmer, uncovered, until
almost all of the cranberries have popped and
the juices are syrupy, about 20 minutes. Transfer
to a container and cool completely. Cover
tightly and refrigerate overnight to marry the
flavors. Remove the cinnamon stick. (The chutney
can be prepared up to 1 week ahead.)

Just before serving, stir in half of the almonds,
and garnish with the rest. Serve chilled or at
room temperature.

Note: *To toast nuts, spread the nuts in a single layer on
a baking sheet. Bake in a preheated 350°F oven, stirring
occasionally, until fragrant and lightly toasted, about
10 minutes. Cool completely before using.*

Roast Turkey with Pan Gravy

Makes 12 to 14 servings

*At least once a year, every family in America finds itself
confronted with the question of how to roast the perfect
turkey. Here's how I do it. With turkeys, like so many
other things, you get what you pay for. Once you've
had a free-range turkey, there's no turning back to the
common variety – free-range birds actually taste like
turkey, and not the artificial flavorings that have been
injected into some brands. I bake the dressing on the
side, and I stuff my bird with vegetables that are only
used as a seasoning (don't serve them). This lighter
stuffing also cuts down on the total roasting time.*

One 14- to 16-pound turkey, preferably
   free-range

8 sprigs of fresh thyme

8 sprigs of fresh sage

1 bay leaf, crumbled

2 medium onions, coarsely chopped

2 medium carrots, coarsely chopped

2 celery ribs, coarsely chopped

1 large leek, white part only, coarsely chopped

Salt and freshly ground black pepper

1/4 cup extra-virgin olive oil

Turkey Broth

Neck and giblets from the turkey
   (save the liver for another use)

2 tablespoons vegetable oil

1 small onion, chopped

1 small celery rib, chopped

3 cups canned low-sodium chicken broth

2 sprigs of fresh thyme or 1/4 teaspoon
   dried thyme

2 sprigs of fresh parsley

1/8 teaspoon whole black peppercorns

1 bay leaf

Gravy

6 cups Turkey Broth

1/4 cup flour dissolved in 1 cup cold water

2 tablespoons unsalted butter, chilled

Salt and freshly ground black pepper

Position a rack in the lower third of the oven and preheat to 375°F.

Rinse the turkey under cold water and pat dry with paper towels. Slip your fingers under the turkey skin, and loosen it at the breast area. Slip 6 sprigs each of thyme and sage under the skin.

Coarsely chop the remaining 2 sprigs each of thyme and sage, and toss with the bay leaf, onions, carrots, celery, and leek in a medium bowl. Season the body cavity with salt and pepper to taste, then loosely stuff with some of the vegetable mixture; cover and refrigerate the remaining vegetables. Place the turkey on a rack in a large roasting pan. Rub all over with the oil, then season the skin with salt and pepper. Cover the breast area only (not the wings or legs) with aluminum foil.

Roast the turkey for 1 hour. Reduce the heat to 325°F and roast for 1 hour more. Remove the foil from the breast, and scatter the remaining vegetables in the pan. Roast until a meat thermometer inserted in the thickest part of the thigh, without touching the bone, reads 180°F. Transfer the turkey to a serving platter and let stand for 20 minutes before carving.

While the turkey is roasting, make the broth. Chop the turkey neck into large chunks with a cleaver or heavy knife. Heat the oil in a large saucepan over medium heat. Add the turkey neck and giblets. Cook, turning occasionally, until well browned, about 10 minutes. Add the onion and celery and cook until softened, about 5 minutes. Stir in the canned broth, scraping up the browned bits on the bottom of the pot. Add enough cold water to cover the ingredients by 2 inches. Bring to a boil over high heat, skimming off the foam that rises to the surface. Reduce the heat to low, and add the thyme, parsley, peppercorns, and bay leaf. Simmer until the broth is well flavored, about 2 hours. Strain the broth. Let stand for 5 minutes, then skim off the fat on the surface.

To make the gravy, discard the vegetables in the roasting pan. Pour the cooking juices into a glass bowl or gravy separator. Let stand 5 minutes, then pour off the fat. Pour the degreased juices back into the roasting pan. Bring to a boil on the stove over high heat, scraping up the browned bits in the pan. Add the broth, then the dissolved cornstarch, and cook until lightly thickened. Remove from the heat and whisk in the butter. Season to taste with salt and pepper and pour into a sauceboat.

Carve the turkey and serve with the gravy.

Cornbread Dressing with Turkey Sausage and Apples

*What other folks call stuffing, I was taught to call dress-
ing, although they are the same thing. (Besides, if my
dressing isn't actually stuffed into the bird, how can it be
called a stuffing?) A couple of important points: First, be
sure that the ingredients are thoroughly cooked before mix-
ing – they will only be heated up in the oven. And let the
bread stand out overnight to become stale so it can hold
more broth without falling apart.*

3 tablespoons vegetable oil

1 pound turkey sausage links, casings removed

2 large onions, chopped

3 Granny Smith apples, peeled, cored,
  and chopped

3 celery ribs, chopped

2 tablespoons poultry seasoning

1 tablespoon chopped fresh sage

2 teaspoons chopped fresh thyme

1 Classic Southern Cornbread (page 74),
  crumbled and left out overnight, uncovered,
  to dry (about 8 cups)

4 cups cubed (1-inch cubes) white sandwich
  bread, left out overnight, uncovered, to dry

3 cups Chicken Broth (page 46) or canned
  low-sodium broth, heated

Salt and freshly ground black pepper

Position a rack in the center of the oven and
preheat to 350°F. Lightly oil a 15 x 10-inch
baking dish.

Heat 1 tablespoon of the oil in a large skillet.
Add the turkey sausage and cook, breaking up
the meat with the side of a spoon, until it loses
its pink color, about 8 minutes. Transfer to a
large bowl.

Add the remaining 2 tablespoons of oil to the
skillet and heat. In batches, if necessary, add the
onions, apples, and celery and cook, stirring often,
until the onions are tender, about 10 minutes.
Stir in the poultry seasoning, sage, and thyme.
Mix with the sausage in the bowl.

Add the cornbread and bread cubes and mix well.
Gradually add enough of the broth to moisten
the dressing; it should not be soggy. Season to
taste with salt and pepper. Spread evenly in
the baking dish and cover tightly with aluminum
foil. (The dressing can be prepared up to 6 hours
ahead and refrigerated.)

Bake until the dressing is heated through, about
30 minutes (about 45 minutes if the dressing
has been chilled). If you like a crusty top, remove
the foil halfway through baking. Serve hot.

Sunday Dinner Pot Roast

Makes 6 servings

Sunday is the time for cooking dishes that require a more leisurely approach. Pot roast certainly falls into that category. Of all the cuts of meat that can be braised, I find that chuck roast or bottom round gives the most succulent results.

4 tablespoons extra-virgin olive oil

One 4-pound boneless beef pot roast

Salt and freshly ground black pepper

1 large onion, coarsely chopped

1 large leek, white part only, coarsely chopped

3 medium carrots, cut into 1-inch pieces

3 celery ribs, cut into 1-inch pieces

2 garlic cloves, minced

1 cup hearty dry red wine, such as
    Zinfandel, optional

2 tablespoons tomato paste

3 cups Beef Broth (page 47) or canned
    low-sodium broth

4 sprigs of fresh thyme or $1/2$ teaspoon
    dried thyme

2 bay leaves

1 pound small new potatoes, scrubbed

3 tablespoons unsalted butter, at
    room temperature

3 tablespoons all-purpose flour

Position a rack in the center of the oven and preheat to 325°F.

Heat 2 tablespoons of the oil in a Dutch oven or flameproof casserole over medium-high heat. Season the beef with salt and pepper to taste. Cook in the pot, turning occasionally, until browned, about 8 minutes. Transfer to a plate.

Add the remaining 2 tablespoons of oil to the pot and heat. Add the onion, leek, carrots, and celery, and cook, stirring often, until softened, about 5 minutes. Add the garlic and cook for 1 minute. Stir in the wine and tomato paste. Cook until evaporated by half, about 3 minutes. Return the meat to the pot and add the broth. Bring to a boil, skimming off any foam that rises to the surface. Add the thyme and bay leaves.

Cover and bake until the meat is fork tender, about 2 hours. Add the potatoes and bake for another 30 minutes.

Transfer the meat to a deep platter, then use a slotted spoon to top with the vegetables. Cover with foil to keep warm. Let the cooking liquid stand for 5 minutes. Skim off any fat on the surface. Mash the butter and flour with a rubber spatula in a medium bowl to make a paste. Gradually whisk about 1 cup of the cooking liquid into the paste, then whisk into the pot. Bring to a simmer over medium heat, stirring often, until thickened, about 5 minutes. Season to taste with salt and pepper.

Pour some of the gravy over the meat and vegetables. Pour the remaining gravy into a sauceboat. Carve the meat and serve with the vegetables, with the gravy passed on the side.

Tropical Pork Roast with Black Beans

Makes 6 servings

Alive with the flavors of the Caribbean, this pork roast has a tart citrus sauce. Sour oranges, which have thick, bumpy skins, are available at Latin markets; substitute a seedless navel orange, if you wish. Cooking the roast in an oven bag makes it so tender you can practically cut it with a spoon.

Marinade

1 orange, preferably sour orange, sliced into
   thick rounds

2 teaspoons crushed cumin seed

2 teaspoons dried oregano

5 garlic cloves, crushed under a knife

1/2 cup fresh orange juice

1/2 cup fresh lime juice

One 3-pound boneless pork butt roast

Black Beans

2 tablespoons extra-virgin olive oil

1/2 cup finely chopped onion

1/2 cup finely chopped green bell pepper

1 teaspoon ground cumin

1 teaspoon dried oregano

2 garlic cloves, minced

3/4 cup Chicken Broth (page 46) or canned
   low-sodium broth

3 Roma or plum tomatoes, seeded and chopped
   into 1/2-inch dice

continued on next page

Tropical Pork Roast with Black Beans continued

Three 15-ounce cans black beans, drained
    and rinsed
Salt and freshly ground black pepper

To make the marinade, place the orange slices,
cumin, oregano, and garlic in a large bowl and
crush the orange slices into the spices with a
large spoon. Stir in the orange and lime juices.
Add the pork and turn to coat on all sides. Cover
and refrigerate for 2 hours.

Position a rack in the center of the oven and
preheat to 325°F.

Transfer the meat and marinade to a plastic oven
bag, cover tightly, and bake until the pork is fork
tender, about 3 hours.

Meanwhile, prepare the black beans. Heat the oil
in a medium saucepan over medium heat. Add
the onion and bell pepper and cook, stirring
often, until softened, about 5 minutes. Add the
cumin, oregano, and garlic and cook for 1
minute. Add the broth and tomatoes and bring
to a simmer. Reduce the heat to low and cook
for 5 minutes. Stir in the black beans and cook
until the flavors are combined, about 10 minutes more. Season to taste with salt and pepper.
Keep warm.

Transfer the pork to a serving platter and cover
with aluminum foil to keep warm. Strain the
cooking liquid into a bowl, pressing hard on the
solids. Let stand for 5 minutes. Skim any fat
from the surface. Season to taste with salt and
pepper. Pour into a sauceboat.

Slice the pork and serve with the sauce and
black beans.

Mushroom, Provolone, and Rosemary Pizza

Makes one 12-inch pizza, 2 to 4 servings

*Seth Roth, Executive Chef of Harpo Studios, helped me
develop this recipe for the website. The recipe makes
enough dough for one medium-size pizza, but it is easy
to multiply the recipe to make more. The dough includes
a sponge, or yeasty batter that adds extra flavor to the
crust. Of course, this mushroom topping is just a suggestion. For a more classic combination, use mozzarella
cheese and Oven-Roasted Tomatoes (page 34), topped with
chopped fresh basil.*

Pizza Dough

1 cup unbleached flour
1/2 cup whole wheat flour
1/2 cup warm (105° to 115°F) water
1 1/4-ounce package active dry yeast
1/2 teaspoon salt
3 tablespoons cold water, as needed

Mushroom Topping

2 tablespoons extra-virgin olive oil
10 ounces cremini or white button
    mushrooms, sliced
2 teaspoons chopped fresh rosemary or
    1 teaspoon dried rosemary
1 garlic clove, minced
Salt and freshly ground black pepper
Yellow cornmeal, for the baker's peel
1 cup (4 ounces) shredded Provolone cheese
1/4 cup freshly grated Parmesan cheese

To make the dough, combine the unbleached flour and whole wheat flour in a small bowl. Stir 1/2 cup of the flour mixture, 1/2 cup of warm water, and the yeast in another small bowl to make a batter. Cover with plastic wrap and let stand until the mixture doubles in volume and bubbles, about 45 minutes.

Pulse the remaining 1 cup of the flour mixture, the yeast mixture, and the salt in a food processor fitted with the metal blade. With the machine running, add the cold water. Process until the dough forms a ball on top of the blade. Feel the dough – if it is too wet, add a tablespoon of unbleached flour and process again. If the dough is too dry, add a tablespoon of cold water and process. To knead the ball of dough, process for 45 seconds.

Remove the dough from the food processor, knead briefly on a lightly floured surface, and form into a ball. Place in a lightly oiled medium bowl and cover tightly with plastic wrap. Let stand in a warm place until doubled in volume, about 45 minutes.

Meanwhile, make the topping. Heat the oil in a medium skillet over medium heat. Add the mushrooms and cook, stirring often, until tender, about 8 minutes. Stir in the rosemary and garlic and cook until the garlic softens, about 2 minutes. Season to taste with salt and pepper.

Position a rack in the lower third of the oven, place a baking stone on the rack, and preheat to 450°F.

Punch down the dough. Roll out on an unfloured surface into a 12-inch round. (If the dough retracts, cover with plastic wrap and let stand for a few minutes, then try again.) Transfer the dough to a baker's peel or rimless baking sheet that has been dusted with cornmeal. Sprinkle with half of the Provolone cheese, then the mushrooms. Top with the remaining Provolone cheese, then the Parmesan.

Slide the pizza onto the stone. Bake until the crust is golden brown, about 15 minutes. Slide the pizza back onto the peel and onto a cutting board. Cut into wedges and serve hot.

Turkey Shepherd's Pie

Serves 8

What is it about a casserole that is so comforting – its sustaining warmth, its unabashed heartiness, or its straightforward flavors? This casserole has all these attributes and more. With its ground turkey filling and mashed potato topping, it is a lightened version of the traditional lamb shepherd's pie.

2 pounds russet potatoes, peeled and cut into 1-inch cubes

2 pounds ground turkey (7% fat content)

1 large yellow onion, minced

2 medium carrots, cut into $1/2$-inch cubes

2 celery ribs, cut into $1/2$-inch cubes

1 clove garlic, minced

One $14^1/2$-ounce can tomatoes, with their juices, chopped

2 cups defrosted frozen peas

1 tablespoon chile powder

1 teaspoon ground cumin

Salt and freshly ground black pepper

$1/2$ cup buttermilk

$1/2$ cup shredded light Cheddar cheese

Position a rack in the top third of the oven and preheat to 350°F.

Place the potatoes in a saucepan with enough lightly salted water to cover by 1-inch. Bring to a boil over medium-high heat and cook until the potatoes are tender, about 15 minutes. Drain and return to the pot.

Meanwhile, cook the ground turkey in a large nonstick skillet over medium heat, breaking up the meat with a spoon, until it loses its pink color, about 7 minutes. Add the onion, carrots, celery, and garlic and cook until the vegetables soften, about 5 minutes. Stir in the tomatoes, peas, chile powder, and cumin and bring to a simmer. Season to taste with salt and pepper.

Spoon the turkey mixture into a 13 x 9-inch baking dish. Mash the potatoes in the pot with the buttermilk and season to taste with salt and pepper. Spread the mashed potatoes over the turkey and sprinkle with the cheese. Bake until the juices are bubbling and until the cheese is melted, 30 to 40 minutes. Serve hot.

Family reunions allow us to connect and reconnect with our relatives and loved ones.

For many of us, the connection between food and tradition is unbreakable. Regardless of your

family make-up, every time you are together is special. Family tradition is practiced daily.

Reunion Chicken and Rice

Makes 6 servings

This homey recipe, which is the star of many a church supper or family reunion, is fine just as it is, but it can be gussied up by adding cooked vegetables – broccoli spears, asparagus tips, or green peas are all great. Stir them into the finished dish, cover, and let stand off the heat for about five minutes to heat the vegetables through. If you are transporting the dish to a covered-dish buffet, do what my mother does: Cook the rice for only fifteen minutes, then add the chicken. Wrap the dish in thick towels and take it with you. The rice will continue to cook in the residual heat of the pot, and stay warm for up to an hour.

One 3- to 3$\frac{1}{2}$-pound chicken, cut into 8 pieces

1 medium onion, chopped

2 celery ribs, chopped

1 bay leaf

2 quarts water

Salt and freshly ground pepper

2 cups long-grain rice

Red Pepper Vinegar (page 35), for serving

Place the chicken, onion, celery, and bay leaf in a 5-quart Dutch oven or covered casserole and add the water, $\frac{1}{2}$ teaspoon salt, and $\frac{1}{4}$ teaspoon pepper. Bring to a boil over high heat, skimming off any foam that rises to the surface. Reduce the heat to low and cover tightly. Simmer, occasionally skimming the broth, until the chicken is tender, about 50 minutes.

Using tongs, transfer the chicken to a platter (keep the broth and vegetables simmering) and cool until easy to handle. Discard the skin and bones and cut the meat into bite-size pieces.

Meanwhile, increase the heat under the broth to high and cook until the liquid is reduced to 4 cups. (If you're in a hurry, strain the broth, reserving the vegetables, and measure 4 cups of broth, reserving the remaining broth for another use. Return the 4 cups of broth and vegetables to the pot.) Skim any fat from the surface of the broth.

Add the rice to the boiling broth and vegetables and return to a boil. Reduce the heat to low and cover tightly. Cook until the rice is almost tender, about 15 minutes. Add the chicken (do not stir) and cook for another 5 minutes, until the rice is tender. Remove from the heat and let stand for 5 minutes.

Stir the chicken into the rice, fluffing the rice at the same time, and season to taste with salt and pepper. Serve hot, with the vinegar for seasoning.

Chicken and Dumplings

Makes 6 servings

Few recipes are more Southern or downright delicious than chicken and dumplings. Most folks won't get any more fancy with seasonings than a little parsley. The truth is that other fresh herbs, like chives, tarragon, or savory, are also good.

One 3- to 3 1/2-pound chicken, cut into 8 pieces

1 medium onion, chopped

2 celery ribs, chopped

2 carrots, sliced into rounds

2 quarts water

Salt and freshly ground black pepper

Dumplings

1 1/2 cups all-purpose flour

Pinch of salt

1/2 cup plus 1 tablespoon water

1 tablespoon canola oil

2 tablespoons chopped fresh parsley, for garnish

Place the chicken, onion, celery, and carrots in a 5-quart Dutch oven or covered casserole and add the water, 1/2 teaspoon salt, and 1/4 teaspoon pepper. Bring to a boil over high heat, skimming off any foam that rises to the surface. Reduce the heat to low and cover tightly. Simmer, occasionally skimming the broth, until the chicken is tender, about 50 minutes.

Using tongs, transfer the chicken to a platter (keep the broth and vegetables simmering) and cool it until it's easy to handle. Discard the skin and bones and cut the meat into bite-size pieces.

Meanwhile, increase the heat under the broth to high and cook until the liquid is reduced to 6 cups. (If you're in a hurry, strain the broth, reserving the vegetables, and measure 6 cups of broth, reserving the remaining broth for another use. Return the 6 cups of broth and vegetables to the pot.) Skim off any fat from the surface of the broth. Stir the chicken back into the pot. Season to taste with salt and pepper.

To make the dumplings, place the flour, salt, and oil in a medium bowl and gradually stir in the water to make a stiff dough. Turn out onto a lightly floured surface and knead briefly. Roll out 1/4-inch thick. Using a sharp knife, cut the dough into 1-inch-wide strips. (If you wish, you can do what my mother does – make the dumpling strips while the chicken is simmering, and freeze the strips until ready to cook.)

Slide the strips into the simmering soup, placing them next to each other without stacking or crowding. Cover tightly and reduce the heat to low. Simmer until the dumplings are cooked through and tender, about 10 minutes.

Sprinkle the dumplings with parsley. Serve from the pot, breaking up the dumplings as needed.

Seven-Layer Salad with Dill-Caper Dressing

Makes 6 to 8 servings

One of the problems with bringing a green salad to pot-lucks is that the vinaigrette wilts the greens by the time the salad gets served. An artful layering of crisp romaine lettuce and other vegetables with a thick herbed dressing solves the problem.

Dressing

1/2 cup mayonnaise, preferably reduced-fat

1/2 cup sour cream, preferably reduced-fat

1 tablespoon Dijon mustard

1 tablespoon chopped fresh dill

1 tablespoon rinsed capers

Salt and coarsely ground black pepper

Hot red pepper sauce

2 romaine hearts, trimmed and torn into bite-size pieces

1/2 pint cherry or grape tomatoes

2 medium carrots, shredded

2 celery ribs, sliced into 1/8 -inch-thick pieces

1 medium sweet red or yellow pepper, seeded and thinly sliced

1 cup fresh corn kernels, blanched in boiling water for 2 minutes, drained, and rinsed

1 seedless cucumber, sliced into 1/8 -inch-thick rounds

To make the dressing, mix the mayonnaise, sour cream, Dijon mustard, dill, and capers in a small bowl. Season to taste with salt, pepper, and hot sauce.

Layer the vegetables in a large glass bowl in the following order: romaine, tomatoes, carrots, celery, red pepper, and corn. Arrange overlapping slices of the cucumber on top. Spread the dressing over the cucumbers.

Cover tightly with plastic wrap and refrigerate until ready to serve, up to 8 hours. Just before serving, toss well.

Chicken and Biscuits

Makes 6 servings

This is a fine dish for a Sunday supper or anytime you're in the mood for comfort food of the first order.

One 3- to 3 1/2-pound chicken, cut into 8 pieces

1 medium onion, chopped

2 celery ribs, chopped

2 medium carrots, cut into 1/2-inch rounds

2 quarts water

Salt and freshly ground black pepper

2 garlic cloves, minced

1 sprig of fresh thyme or 1/4 teaspoon fresh
    thyme leaves

1 sprig of fresh parsley

1 bay leaf

6 tablespoons (3/4 stick) unsalted butter,
    softened

1/3 cup plus 1 tablespoon all-purpose flour

2 medium red-skinned potatoes, peeled and
    cut into 1/2-inch cubes

3 ounces green beans, cut into 1/2-inch lengths

1 cup fresh or frozen butter or lima beans

Dough for Boarding House Biscuits (page 76)

Place the chicken, onion, celery, and carrots in a 5-quart Dutch oven or covered casserole and add the water, 1/2 teaspoon salt, and 1/4 teaspoon pepper. Bring to a boil over high heat, skimming off any foam that rises to the surface. Add the garlic, thyme, parsley, and bay leaf. Reduce the

heat to low and cover tightly. Simmer, occasionally skimming the broth, until the chicken is tender, about 50 minutes.

Using tongs, transfer the chicken to a platter (keep the broth and vegetables simmering) and cool until easy to handle. Discard the skin and bones and cut the meat into bite-size pieces.

Meanwhile, increase the heat under the broth to high and cook until the liquid is reduced to 6 cups. (If you're in a hurry, strain the broth, discarding the vegetables, and measure 6 cups of broth, reserving the remaining broth for another use. Return the 6 cups of broth to the pot.) Skim off any fat from the surface of the broth.

Mash the butter and flour in a medium bowl with a rubber spatula to make a paste. Gradually whisk in about 2 cups of the broth, then whisk this mixture back into the pot. Bring to a boil over medium heat, whisking almost constantly. Stir the chicken back into the pot, then add the potatoes, carrots, green beans, and butter beans. Season to taste with salt and pepper. Remove from the heat and set aside.

Position a rack in the center of the oven and preheat to 400°F. Drop 12 mounds of the biscuit dough over the chicken and sauce. Bake until the biscuits are golden brown and a toothpick inserted in the center biscuit comes out clean, 30 to 40 minutes. Serve hot.

Sweet Potato Salad with Pineapple and Red Peppers

Makes 8 servings

For an interesting twist to the tried-and-true potato salad, try this version made with sweet potatoes and pineapple. I can't think of a better match for spareribs or baked ham. The yellow-fleshed "true" sweet potatoes aren't as flavorful as orange Louisiana or jewel yams.

4 orange-fleshed yams (sweet potatoes)

1/4 cup mayonnaise, regular or reduced-fat

2 tablespoons Dijon mustard

4 celery ribs, cut into 1/4-inch-
 thick slices

1 small red bell pepper, seeded and cut into
 1/4-inch dice

1 cup diced (1/2-inch) ripe fresh pineapple

2 scallions, white and green parts,
 finely chopped

Salt and freshly ground pepper

1/2 cup (2 ounces) coarsely chopped
 pecans, toasted

Chopped fresh chives, for garnish

Following the directions on page 91, roast the yams until tender. Cool until easy to handle. Peel, then cut into 3/4-inch chunks.

In a large bowl, mix the mayonnaise and mustard. Add the yams, celery, red pepper, pineapple, and scallions and toss gently, seasoning to taste with salt and pepper. Cover and refrigerate until chilled, about 1 hour. (The salad can be made 1 day ahead, covered, and refrigerated. Adjust the seasonings before serving.)

Just before serving, fold in the pecans and sprinkle with the chives. Serve chilled.

Old-Fashioned Potato Salad

Makes 6 to 8 servings

This is the way my mother, Addie Mae, has made her potato salad at just about every family get-together for as long as I can remember. She likes tender celery, so she cooks it along with the potatoes.

2 pounds Yukon Gold potatoes, peeled and cut
 into 3/4-inch cubes

1/2 medium onion, chopped (about 1/2 cup)

4 celery ribs, sliced into 1/2-inch-thick half-moons

1 teaspoon salt

4 large eggs, boiled and peeled

1 cup Homemade Mayonnaise (page 32)
 or store-bought mayonnaise

1/4 cup sweet pickle relish

2 tablespoons cider vinegar

1 teaspoon yellow mustard

Salt and freshly ground pepper

Chopped fresh parsley and sweet paprika,
 for garnish

Place the potatoes, onion, celery, and salt in a large saucepan and add enough water to cover by 1 inch. Bring to a boil over medium-high heat. Reduce the heat to low. Simmer until the potatoes are tender, about 15 minutes. Drain.

Peel and slice the hard-boiled eggs.

Whisk the mayonnaise, relish, vinegar, and mustard in a large bowl. Add the cooked vegetables and hard-boiled eggs and mix. Season to taste with salt and pepper. Garnish with chopped parsley and paprika. Cover and refrigerate until well chilled, at least 2 hours.

Perfect Cream Cheese Piecrust

Makes one 9-inch piecrust

Every cook wants to have the recipe for the perfect pie-crust. I've baked plenty in my time, but this is the easiest to make with the best results. It isn't as flaky as shortening-based piecrusts, but it is tasty, golden brown, and crisp.

3 ounces cream cheese (not reduced-fat),
   at room temperature

6 tablespoons (^{3}/4 stick) unsalted butter,
   at room temperature

^{3}/4 cup all-purpose flour

1 tablespoon sugar

^{1}/4 teaspoon salt

Mix the cream cheese and butter in a medium bowl with a hand-held mixer on low speed. Add the flour, sugar, and salt and mix just until the dough clumps together. (The dough may look crumbly, but it will hold together when pressed.) Gather into a thick disk, wrap in plastic wrap, and refrigerate for at least 1 hour. If the dough is refrigerated longer than 1 hour and becomes firm, let stand at room temperature for 10 minutes before rolling out.

Variation

Double Crust Perfect Pie Dough: Use 8 ounces cream cheese, 1 cup (2 sticks) unsalted butter, 2 cups all-purpose flour, 2 tablespoons sugar, and ^{1}/2 teaspoon salt. Divide the dough into 2 thick disks, one slightly larger than the other.

French Chocolate-Almond Pie

Makes 8 servings

My friend Schomburger, caterer extraordinaire, taught me this recipe when I worked for Governor Bob Graham of Florida. I make it for very special parties and large crowds because it is easy to make.

Crust

1 cup all-purpose flour

1/2 cup (1 1/2 ounces) sliced almonds

1/3 cup (packed) light brown sugar

6 tablespoons (3/4 stick) unsalted butter, chilled, cut into pieces

1 large egg yolk beaten with 1 tablespoon water

Filling

2 ounces unsweetened chocolate, finely chopped

12 tablespoons (1 1/2 sticks) unsalted butter, at room temperature

1 cup plus 2 tablespoons granulated sugar

3 large eggs, beaten lightly

1 teaspoon vanilla extract

1/2 teaspoon almond extract

1 cup heavy cream

2 tablespoons confectioners' sugar

1/4 cup sliced almonds, toasted

To make the crust, position a rack in the center of the oven and preheat to 350°F. Lightly butter a 9-inch pie pan.

Process the flour, almonds, and brown sugar together in a food processor fitted with the metal blade (or in batches in a blender) until the almonds are very finely ground into a powder. Add the butter and pulse until the mixture is crumbly. With the machine running, add the egg yolk and pulse just until the dough clumps together. Roll out the dough on a lightly floured surface. Transfer to the pan and press it in (it will probably crack in the transfer). Prick the dough well with a fork, and freeze for 10 minutes.

Bake until the crust is golden brown, about 18 minutes. Transfer to a wire rack and cool completely.

To make the filling, melt the chocolate and butter in the top part of a double boiler over hot but not simmering water. Add sugar and stir. Add the eggs, vanilla, and almond extracts. Stirring constantly, cook till the mixture coats the back of a spoon, about 10 minutes. (The egg mixture must reach 160 degrees to be safe.) Remove from the heat and chill in an ice bath and then refrigerate.

To finish the filling, beat the cream and sugar with a hand-held mixer on high speed until stiff peaks form. Remove custard from the refrigerator and whisk until light. Gently fold in the cream and pour into shell. Garnish with sliced almonds and chill well.

Chocolate Pecan Pie

Makes 8 servings

Whoever first thought of adding chocolate to pecan pie deserves a place in the Dessert Hall of Fame. Serve this with a big dollop of whipped cream or vanilla ice cream.

Perfect Cream Cheese Piecrust (page 203)

2 ounces unsweetened chocolate,

    finely chopped

1^1/2 cups sugar

1 cup light corn syrup

3 large eggs

2 tablespoons unsalted butter, melted

1 teaspoon vanilla extract or ^{1}/2 teaspoon

    rum extract

^{1}/4 teaspoon salt

1^1/2 cups pecan halves, coarsely chopped

^{1}/2 cup pecan halves, whole

Sweetened whipped cream or vanilla ice

    cream, for serving

Position a rack in the bottom third of the oven and preheat to 350°F.

On a lightly floured surface, roll out the dough into a ^{1}/8-inch-thick circle. Fold in half and place in a 9-inch pie pan. Unfold and fit into the pan. Fold the edges of the dough over so they are flush with the edge of the pan and flute the edges. Freeze for 15 minutes.

Melt the chocolate in the top part of a double boiler over hot but not simmering water. (Or microwave on Medium, stirring occasionally, until melted, about 2 minutes.) Cool until tepid.

Whisk the sugar, corn syrup, eggs, chocolate, butter, vanilla, and salt until combined. Add the chopped pecans. Pour into the pie shell. Arrange the whole pecan halves on top of the filling in concentric circles. Place the pie on a baking sheet.

Bake until the filling is evenly puffed (the filling may seem slightly underset in the center), 50 minutes to 1 hour.

Transfer to a wire rack and cool until warm or cool completely. Cut into wedges and serve with the whipped cream.

Southern Sweet Potato Pie

Makes 8 servings

Every Southern baker worth his or her salt has a recipe for sweet potato pie. This one is as good as they come, nice and smooth and gently spiced.

Perfect Cream Cheese Piecrust (page 203)

2 cups mashed cooked sweet potatoes (about 2 1/4 pounds), puréed in a food processor or blender (see Note, page 91)

3 large eggs, lightly beaten

1 cup granulated sugar

1/4 cup (firmly packed) light brown sugar

1/4 cup half-and-half

3 tablespoons unsalted butter, melted

1 tablespoon fresh lemon juice

1 teaspoon vanilla extract

1 teaspoon ground cinnamon

1/2 teaspoon freshly ground nutmeg

1/2 teaspoon salt

Grated zest of 1 lemon

Sweetened whipped cream, for serving

On a lightly floured surface, roll out the dough into a 1/8-inch-thick circle. Fold in half and place in a 9-inch pie pan. Unfold and fit into the pan. Fold the edges of the dough over so they are flush with the edge of the pan and flute the edges. Freeze for 15 minutes.

Position a rack in the center of the oven and preheat to 400°F.

Mix the sweet potatoes, eggs, granulated and brown sugars, half-and-half, melted butter, lemon juice, vanilla, cinnamon, nutmeg, salt, and lemon zest with a hand-held electric mixer on low speed until smooth.

Bake for 20 minutes. Reduce the oven temperature to 325°F and bake until the outer edges are puffed and a knife inserted 1 inch from the center comes out clean, about 1 hour. Transfer to a wire rack to cool completely. Serve with sweetened whipped cream.

Creamy Custard Pie

Makes 8 servings

In the pie world, custard pie has a delicate personality all its own. This recipe uses half-and-half to make the filling a bit richer than most.

Perfect Cream Cheese Piecrust (page 203)

4 large eggs, 3 whole and 1 separated

2 cups half-and-half

2/3 cup sugar

1 teaspoon vanilla extract

About 1/4 teaspoon freshly grated nutmeg

On a lightly floured surface, roll out the dough into a 1/8-inch-thick circle. Fold in half and place in a 9-inch pie pan. Unfold and fit into the pan. Fold the edges of the dough over so they are flush with the edge of the pan and flute the edges. Freeze for 15 minutes.

Position a rack in the center of the oven and preheat to 400°F.

Place the pan on a baking sheet. Line the pan with aluminum foil and fill with pastry weights or raw rice. Bake until the dough looks set, about 12 minutes. Remove from the oven and lift off the foil with the weights.

Lightly beat the egg white until frothy. Brush some of the white on the bottom and sides of the pie shell. Bake until the brushed area looks dry, about 3 minutes.

Whisk the 3 whole eggs with the egg yolk, half-and-half, sugar, and vanilla. Pour into the pie shell and sprinkle with the nutmeg.

Bake for 10 minutes. Reduce the heat to 325°F and continue baking until a knife inserted 1 inch from the center comes out clean, about 35 to 45 minutes. Transfer to a wire rack and cool completely.

Strawberry-Rhubarb Pie

Makes 8 servings

I don't know many people who enjoy rhubarb all by itself, but it sure is good when mixed with strawberries and turned into pie. In fact, as fruit pies go, it's one of the best, and something that isn't served as often as it should be.

Double Crust Perfect Pie Dough (page 203)

1 1/4 pounds rhubarb, cut into 1/2 inch

   half-moons (about 4 cups)

1 pint strawberries, quartered (about 2 cups)

1 cup plus 1 tablespoon sugar

1/3 cup all-purpose flour

1 teaspoon vanilla extract

Grated zest of 1 lemon

1 large egg white, lightly beaten with

   1 teaspoon water

Sweetened whipped cream, for serving

Position a rack in the center of the oven and preheat to 400°F.

On a lightly floured surface, roll out the larger disk of dough into a 1/8-inch-thick circle. Fold in half and place in a 9-inch pie pan. Unfold and fit into the pan. Refrigerate while making the filling.

Gently toss together the rhubarb, strawberries, 1 cup of sugar, flour, vanilla, and lemon zest. Let stand for 15 minutes, or until the fruit begins to release its juices. Pour into the pie shell.

Roll the second disk of dough into a 1/8-inch-thick circle. Using a pizza or pastry wheel or a sharp knife, cut the dough into 3/4-inch-wide strips. Arrange the strips across the top of the pie in a lattice pattern. Fold the edges of the bottom crust over the ends of the strips and flute the edges. Brush the lattice strips lightly with some of the beaten egg white and sprinkle with the remaining 1 tablespoon of sugar. Place the pie on a baking sheet.

Bake for 10 minutes. Reduce the oven temperature to 350°F and bake until the juices in the center of the pie are bubbling, about 45 to 55 minutes. Transfer to a wire rack and cool completely.

Raisin Bread Pudding with Orange Butterscotch Sauce

Makes 8 servings

This is an extraordinary bread pudding. Try to use a flavorful egg bread, such as challah or brioche or at least a firm white sandwich bread – fluffy, tasteless bread need not apply. And the orange butterscotch sauce is a winner! If you wish, substitute additional fresh orange juice for the liqueur.

Bread Pudding

2 tablespoons unsalted butter, plus more
   for the pan

2 Golden Delicious apples, peeled, cored,
   and cut into $3/4$-inch cubes

$1/4$ cup plus 2 tablespoons (packed) light
   brown sugar

$1^1/2$ cups heavy cream

$1^1/2$ cups milk

$3/4$ cup granulated sugar

3 whole eggs

6 egg yolks

2 teaspoons vanilla extract

1 teaspoon ground cinnamon

8 cups (1-inch cubes) egg bread, such as
   challah or brioche (1 pound)

$1/2$ cup raisins

Orange Butterscotch Sauce

3 tablespoons unsalted butter

$1/4$ cup plus 2 tablespoons (packed) light
   brown sugar

$1/4$ cup plus 2 tablespoons orange-flavored
   liqueur, such as Grand Marnier

$1/4$ cup plus 2 tablespoons fresh orange juice

Grated zest of 1 orange

$1/4$ cup plus 2 tablespoons heavy cream

Position a rack in the center of the oven and preheat to 350°F. Lightly butter an $11^1/2$ x 8-inch baking dish.

To make the pudding, heat the butter in a large skillet over medium-high heat. Add the apples and cook, stirring occasionally, until they begin to brown, about 5 minutes. Add 2 tablespoons of the brown sugar and stir until the apples are coated with the melted sugar, about 1 minute. Set aside.

Whisk the cream, milk, granulated sugar, remaining $1/4$ cup brown sugar, eggs, egg yolks, vanilla, and cinnamon in a large bowl. Add the bread cubes and raisins and stir. Let stand, stirring often so the bread soaks up the custard evenly, for 15 minutes. Spread half of the bread mixture evenly in the pan. Top with the apples, then spoon the remaining bread mixture over the apples, covering them as best as you can (don't worry if some of the apples peek through). Bake until a knife inserted in the center of the pudding comes out clean, about 1 hour.

Meanwhile, make the sauce. Melt the butter and brown sugar together in a medium saucepan over medium heat, stirring often. Stir in the liqueur, orange juice and zest, and cream. Bring to a boil. Cook until the sauce is thickened and reduced to about 1 cup. Keep warm.

Serve the pudding with the warm sauce.

Banana Pudding

Makes 8 servings

You simply cannot find a family-style restaurant in the South that doesn't serve banana pudding. For good reason – it is everything a dessert should be, plus it has the advantage of being easy. While most cooks use vanilla pudding mix, I always make my own pudding with vanilla beans. Another little trick I've learned over the years is to substitute different cookies for the wafers. Here I use vanilla wafers, but some of my very best puddings have been made with home-baked cookies, such as Pecan Shortbread Cookies (page 258).

3 cups milk

2 vanilla beans, split lengthwise

3/4 cup sugar

2 tablespoons plus 1 teaspoon cornstarch

Pinch of salt

6 large egg yolks

2 tablespoons unsalted butter, cut up

12 ounces vanilla wafers

5 ripe bananas, peeled and cut into
  1/4-inch-thick rounds

1 cup heavy cream

2 tablespoons confectioners' sugar

Bring the milk and vanilla beans to a simmer in a medium saucepan over low heat. Using tongs, remove the beans from the milk. Using the tip of a small sharp knife, scrape the tiny seeds from each bean back into the milk.

Whisk the sugar, cornstarch, and salt in a medium bowl. Add the egg yolks and whisk well. Gradually whisk in about half of the hot milk, then pour the yolk mixture into the saucepan. Cook over medium heat, stirring constantly, until the pudding comes to a full boil. Remove from the heat and whisk in the butter until melted. Transfer to a medium bowl. Cover the pudding with a piece of plastic wrap pressed directly onto the surface and pierce a few holes in the wrap with the tip of a knife. Let stand until tepid, about 30 minutes.

Spoon about 1 cup of the pudding into a 2- to 2 1/2-quart glass bowl. Layer the cookies, bananas, and pudding in the bowl, ending with the pudding. Cover tightly and refrigerate until chilled, at least 4 hours or overnight.

Whip the cream and confectioners' sugar in a chilled medium bowl until stiff. Spread the whipped cream over the pudding. Serve chilled, spooned into bowls.

Peach Buckle

Makes 4 to 6 servings

My friend Adelaide Suber likes to make her cobblers with a cake topping, which makes folks think it should be called a buckle. I don't care what you call it – we're talking about juicy summer peaches sitting under a sweet yellow cake layer. Serve it warm with vanilla ice cream, and you'll be in heaven.

Filling

2 pounds ripe peaches, peeled, pitted, and
   sliced (5 cups)

$1/2$ cup (packed) light brown sugar

$1/4$ cup all-purpose flour

2 tablespoons unsalted butter, cut up

$1/4$ teaspoon ground cinnamon

Topping

1 cup all-purpose flour

$1/2$ teaspoon baking powder

$1/2$ teaspoon baking soda

$1/8$ teaspoon salt

6 tablespoons ($3/4$ stick) unsalted butter, at
   room temperature

$1/2$ cup granulated sugar

1 large egg, at room temperature (see Note,
   page 32)

$1/2$ teaspoon vanilla extract

$1/2$ teaspoon almond extract

$1/2$ cup buttermilk

Position a rack in the center of the oven and preheat to 350°F. Lightly butter an 11 x 8$1/2$-inch glass or ceramic baking dish.

To make the filling, toss the peaches, brown sugar, cinnamon, flour, and butter in a medium bowl. Transfer to the baking dish.

To make the topping, whisk the flour, baking powder, baking soda, and salt in a medium bowl to combine. Beat the butter and sugar in a medium bowl with a hand-held electric mixer on high speed until light in color and texture, about 3 minutes. Beat in the egg, vanilla, and almond extract. On low speed, add the flour in 3 additions, alternating with 2 additions of the buttermilk, beginning and ending with the flour, and mix until smooth, scraping down the sides of the bowl often with a rubber spatula. Spread the batter over the peaches.

Bake until a toothpick inserted in the center of the topping comes out clean, about 45 minutes. Cool slightly. Serve warm or cooled to room temperature.

Pear and Cranberry Cobbler

Makes 6 servings

Bakers often disagree about what topping should be used for a cobbler. Should it be pie dough or sweet biscuits? There is another camp that uses cake batter, but that is officially called a buckle – see my Peach Buckle (page 212). I use biscuits, but I crisscross strips of the dough into an attractive lattice topping. The pear and cranberry filling makes this a good choice for an autumn celebration.

4 firm ripe Bosc pears, peeled, cored, and sliced
    into $1/2$-inch-wide wedges (about 5 cups)

1 cup fresh or frozen cranberries

$1/2$ cup sugar

1 tablespoon cornstarch

1 teaspoon ground cinnamon

$1/2$ teaspoon ground ginger

Cobbler Topping

$1^1/2$ cups all-purpose flour

$2^1/4$ teaspoons baking powder

$2^1/2$ tablespoons sugar

$1/8$ teaspoon salt

3 tablespoons unsalted butter, chilled, cut up

3 tablespoons vegetable shortening

$1/2$ cup buttermilk, as needed

Position a rack in the center of the oven and preheat to 350°F. Lightly butter an 8-inch square baking dish.

Toss the pears, cranberries, sugar, cornstarch, cinnamon, and ginger in a large bowl. Transfer to the baking dish.

To make the cobbler topping, combine the flour, baking powder, $1^1/2$ tablespoons of the sugar, and salt in a medium bowl. Add the butter and shortening and cut in with a pastry blender or 2 knives until the mixture looks like coarse breadcrumbs. Stir in enough buttermilk to make a soft dough.

Using floured hands, pat out the dough on a floured work surface into an 8-inch square. Using a sharp knife, cut into $3/4$-inch-wide ribbons. Crisscross the dough on the filling in a lattice pattern. Sprinkle the remaining 1 tablespoon of sugar over the dough.

Bake until the cobbler crust is golden brown and the filling juices are bubbling, about 45 minutes. Serve warm.

As a child growing up in rural Florida, I learned the importance of the family table. It was there

that I felt love matched only by my family's appreciation for fresh, wholesome food.

Pear, Ginger, and Pecan Loaf

Makes 8 servings

Everyone needs a recipe for a quick bread that is simple enough to make on a whim but elegant enough for company. This little cake, with chunks of fragrant pear, crystallized ginger, and toasted pecans is perfect for any occasion. Use a firm-ripe Bosc pear, which holds its shape well after baking.

2 cups all-purpose flour

2 teaspoons baking powder

$1/2$ teaspoon baking soda

$1/8$ teaspoon salt

$3/4$ cup sugar

$1/2$ cup pear or apple juice

$1/3$ cup vegetable oil

2 large eggs, beaten

1 large Bosc pear (about 8 ounces), peeled, cored, and cut into $1/2$-inch cubes

$1/2$ cup coarsely chopped pecans, toasted

$1/4$ cup minced crystallized ginger

Position a rack in the center of the oven and preheat to 350°F. Lightly butter and flour an $8 1/2$ x $4 1/2$ x $2 1/2$-inch loaf pan and tap out the excess flour.

In a medium bowl, whisk the flour, baking powder, baking soda, and salt to combine. In another bowl, whisk the sugar, pear juice, oil, and eggs until well mixed. Pour into the dry ingredients and whisk just until smooth. Fold in the pear, pecans, and ginger. Scrape into the pan and smooth the top.

Bake until a toothpick inserted in the center of the cake comes out clean, 45 to 50 minutes. Cool on a wire rack for 10 minutes. Unmold the cake and cool completely.

Banana-Chocolate Chip Cake

Makes 10 to 12 servings

Bananas and chocolate are a tasty match. Adding chocolate chips to banana bread takes it to another level.

2 cups sugar

1 cup (2 sticks) unsalted butter, at room
   temperature

4 large eggs

2 cups mashed, well-ripened bananas

2^1/2 cups self-rising flour

2 cups (12 ounces) semisweet chocolate chips

Position a rack in the lower third of the oven and preheat to 350°F. Butter and flour a 10-inch fluted tube (Bundt) pan, and tap out the excess flour.

Beat the sugar and butter together in a large bowl with a hand-held electric mixer on high speed until light in color and texture. Beat in the eggs, one at a time, beating well after each addition. Reduce to low speed and beat in the bananas. Gradually beat in the dry ingredients, beating just until combined. Mix in the chocolate chips. Spread evenly in the pan.

Bake until a wooden toothpick inserted in the center comes out clean and the cake starts to pull away from the edges of the pan, about 1 hour.

Transfer to a wire rack and cool for 10 minutes. Invert onto the rack and cool completely. (The cake can be prepared up to 2 days ahead, wrapped in plastic wrap, and stored at room temperature.)

Spicy Zucchini Quick Bread

Makes 12 servings

Play around with the spices for this all-American favorite. Sure, you can use ground cinnamon, but there might be other candidates in the spice cabinet. Try Chinese five-spice powder or pumpkin pie spice to add an aromatic lift to this moist quick bread.

3 cups all-purpose flour

2 teaspoons five-spice powder, pumpkin pie
   spice, or ground cinnamon

1 teaspoon baking powder

1 teaspoon baking soda

^{1}/4 teaspoon salt

2 cups sugar

1 cup vegetable oil

3 large eggs

2 teaspoons vanilla extract

2 cups shredded unpeeled zucchini (2 large)

1 cup chopped pecans

Position a rack in the lower third of the oven and preheat to 350°F. Butter and flour a 10-inch fluted tube (Bundt) pan and tap out the excess flour.

Whisk the flour, five-spice powder, baking powder, baking soda, and salt in a large bowl. Make a well in the center. In another bowl, whisk the sugar, oil, eggs, and vanilla and pour into the well. Mix well, then stir in the zucchini and chopped pecans. Spread evenly in the pan.

Bake until a wooden toothpick inserted in the center of the cake comes out clean, about 1 hour.

Transfer to a wire rack and cool for 10 minutes. Invert onto the rack and cool completely. (The cake can be prepared up to 2 days ahead, wrapped in plastic wrap, and stored at room temperature.)

Blueberry Crisp

Makes 6 servings

This is a summertime dessert that you can make with your eyes closed. I love desserts that are this easy and taste this good!

Filling

4 pints fresh blueberries

1/2 cup granulated sugar

2 tablespoons all-purpose flour

Grated zest of 1 lemon

Topping

1 cup all-purpose flour

1/3 cup (packed) light brown sugar

1/3 cup granulated sugar

6 tablespoons (3/4 stick) unsalted butter,
   cut up, at room temperature

Position a rack in the center of the oven and preheat to 400°F. Lightly butter an 11 x 8 1/2-inch glass or ceramic baking dish.

To make the filling, toss the blueberries, sugar, flour, and lemon zest in a large bowl. Pour into the baking dish.

To make the topping, mix the flour and brown and granulated sugar in a medium bowl. Add the butter. Using your fingers, work the ingredients together until thoroughly combined and crumbly. Sprinkle evenly over the filling.

Bake until the berries are bubbling throughout and the topping is golden, about 35 minutes. Serve warm or cooled to room temperature.

Food as Love

Few of us think of food only in times of celebration.
We also think of it in times of sadness and need.
Cooking for others is a way to extend your heart.

When loved ones, friends, or neighbors suffer a loss or when a family member is ill, we arrive at their door with platters and bowls of food. This is one way we show our love and care.

Modern science has developed medicines that cure much of what ails us, but few pills or shots can bring as much comfort as steaming hot soup or rich chocolate cake. Consider Chicken Soup. It's a time-honored antidote to the common cold in Jewish culture. When you eat a bowl and realize how much better you feel afterward, you'll be an immediate chicken soup convert, as I was. I love the expression on people's faces when I show up with a Mason jar of soup. It's better than a big hug!

The healing power of food hit home for me when I visited my grandparents in a nursing home. I arrived as they were finishing supper. My grandmother's face lit up when she tasted the ripe, sweet peach on her tray. I realized how powerful food is, regardless of your stage of life or circumstance. We rely on it for our very existence, and it gives us enormous pleasure.

When someone dies, we bring food. Children find this practice odd – I know I did when, as a young boy, I lost my great-grandmother. The family gathered and on the table appeared copious amounts of wonderful food. I was puzzled by the abundance, but today I realize this is a centuries-old tradition in nearly every culture.

I also find it interesting to note what people bring to a home in mourning. They tote dishes such as Macaroni and Cheese, and Chocolate Cake. Each of these is a great comfort food.

Everyone needs this kind of food at times. The soft texture and mild cheesy flavor of macaroni and cheese is reminiscent of our childhood meals, when we felt safe and cared for. The indulgent sweetness of chocolate cake reminds us of the sweetness of life. As these foods heal our spirit, they bring comfort to our soul.

Summer Squash and Lemon Thyme Soup

Makes 8 servings

This light-bodied soup has a refreshing lemon accent. If you can't find lemon thyme, use regular fresh thyme plus two wide strips of lemon zest, removed from the lemon with a vegetable peeler. This is great for freezing or to give as a gift.

2 tablespoons extra-virgin olive oil

2 medium-size sweet onions, such as Vidalia, finely chopped

1 medium leek, white part only, finely chopped and well rinsed to remove grit

6 garlic cloves, minced

4 medium yellow squash, scrubbed but unpeeled, trimmed and coarsely chopped

4 sprigs of fresh lemon thyme

6 cups Chicken Broth (page 46) or low-sodium canned broth

2 tablespoons fresh lemon juice, or more to taste

Salt

Hot red pepper sauce

Parmesan cheese curls, for garnish (see Note)

1/4 cup pine nuts, for garnish

Freshly grated lemon zest, for garnish

Heat the oil in a soup pot over medium heat. Add the onions, leek, and garlic and cook, stirring often, until the onions are soft and translucent, about 10 minutes.

Add the squash and thyme and cook, stirring often, until the squash begins to soften, about 5 minutes. Add the broth and bring to a boil. Reduce the heat to low. Simmer, partially covered, until the squash is tender, about 20 minutes.

Discard the thyme and purée two thirds of the soup in batches in a covered blender. Return to the soup pot and heat through. Season the soup with lemon juice, salt, and hot pepper sauce.

Ladle into soup bowls and top with the cheese curls, pine nuts, and lemon zest. Serve hot.

Note: *To make Parmesan cheese curls, start with a large chunk of Parmesan cheese. Using a swivel-blade vegetable peeler (the sturdier the better), work directly over each serving of soup, pressing firmly to shave off curls from a flat surface of the cheese.*

Garden Vegetable-Beef Soup

Makes 8 to 12 servings

My grandfather had a green thumb to match my grand-mother's cooking expertise, and the soup she would make from his garden was a wonder to behold. The short ribs are supposed to add just a bit of flavor to the soup, so don't think it would be better to add more – let the vegetables shine through.

1 tablespoon extra-virgin olive oil

1 pound short ribs

Salt and freshly ground black pepper

1 large onion, chopped

2 medium carrots, chopped

2 celery ribs, chopped

2 garlic cloves, minced

2 quarts water

2 sprigs of fresh thyme or $1/4$ teaspoon
    dried thyme

1 bay leaf

4 Roma or plum tomatoes, peeled
    and seeded (see Note, page 30)

1 medium red-skinned potatoes, scrubbed
    and cut into $1/2$-inch dice

1 medium turnip, scrubbed and cut into
    $1/2$-inch dice

1 cup fresh or frozen butter or lima beans

1 cup corn kernels (from 2 ears)

Heat the oil in a large soup pot over high heat. Season the short ribs with salt and pepper to taste. Cook in the oil, turning occasionally, until browned on all sides, about 8 minutes.

Transfer the short ribs to a plate.

Add the onion, carrots, and celery and cook, stirring occasionally, until softened, about 3 minutes. Add the garlic and cook for 1 minute. Return the short ribs to the pot and add the water. Bring to a boil, skimming off any foam that rises to the surface. Add the thyme and bay leaf. Reduce the heat to low and simmer until the short ribs are tender, occasionally skimming fat from the surface, about $2^{1}/2$ hours.

Add the tomatoes, potatoes, turnip, beans, and corn. Continue cooking until the turnip is tender, about 20 minutes. Season to taste with salt and pepper.

Remove from the heat and let stand 5 minutes. Remove and discard the thyme sprigs and bay leaf. Skim the fat from the surface. Serve hot.

Chicken Noodle Soup

Makes 12 to 14 servings

Recipes for great chicken soup usually include some pre-viously made chicken broth. Broth is long-simmered to extract every bit of flavor from the meat and vegetables, which are then thrown away.

With soup, you want these ingredients to retain their flavor and texture. Of course, the best chicken soup is made with homemade chicken broth, but if you use canned broth, I won't tell anyone. This makes a lot of soup, which is fine, because you'll wish you had made a lot anyway.

2 tablespoons vegetable oil

2 medium onions, chopped

3 medium carrots, cut into $1/4$-inch rounds

3 celery ribs, cut into $1/4$-inch-thick slices

One 6- to 7-pound chicken

2 quarts Chicken Broth (page 46) or
  canned low-sodium broth

1 quart cold water, or as needed

4 sprigs of fresh parsley

3 sprigs of fresh thyme or $1/2$ teaspoon
  dried thyme

1 bay leaf

Salt and freshly ground black pepper

2 cups egg noodles

Chopped fresh parsley, for garnish

Heat the oil in a brothpot over medium heat.
Add the onions, carrots, and celery and cook,
stirring often, until softened, about 10 minutes.

Cut the chicken into 8 pieces. If there are any
pads of yellow fat in the tail area, do not remove
them. Add the chicken to the pot and pour in
the broth. Add enough cold water to cover the
ingredients by 2 inches. Bring to a boil over
high heat, skimming off the foam that rises to
the surface. Add the parsley, thyme, and bay leaf.

Reduce the heat to low. Simmer, uncovered,
until the chicken is very tender, about 2 hours.

Remove the chicken from the pot and set aside
until cool enough to handle. Remove and discard
the parsley and thyme sprigs and bay leaf. Let
stand 5 minutes and degrease the soup, reserving
the fat if you are making matzo balls.

Discard the chicken skin and bones and cut the
meat into bite-size pieces. Add the noodles and
cook until done, about 10 minutes. Stir the meat
back into the soup and season to taste with salt
and pepper. Serve hot. (The soup can be prepared
up to 3 days ahead, cooled, covered, and refrigerated, or frozen for up to 3 months.)

Yellow Squash Casserole

Makes 4 to 6 servings

*This is a lightened version of a Southern favorite, squash
casserole. Use zucchini, if you like, or another herb, such
as dill or basil.*

3 medium yellow squash, cut into
  $1/2$-inch half-moons

1 medium onion, chopped

2 garlic cloves, minced

$1/2$ cup Chicken Broth (page 46) or
  canned low-sodium broth

$1 1/2$ cups reduced-fat sour cream

1 teaspoon chopped fresh oregano

Salt and freshly ground black pepper

1 cup fresh breadcrumbs (make in
  the blender or food processor)

1 tablespoon extra-virgin olive oil

Position a rack in the center of the oven and
preheat to 350°F. Lightly oil an 8-inch square
baking dish.

Bring the squash, onion, garlic, and broth to a
boil in a medium saucepan. Cook, stirring
occasionally, until the broth evaporates and the
squash is tender, about 10 minutes. Drain,
and cool slightly. Stir in the sour cream and
oregano and season to taste with salt and
pepper. Spread in the baking dish. Sprinkle with
breadcrumbs and drizzle with the oil.

Bake until the juices are simmering and the
top is crusty, about 30 minutes. Let stand for 5
minutes, then serve hot.

Foods heal our spirit, and bring comfort to our soul.

Auntie's Chocolate Cake with Chocolate-Pecan Frosting

Makes 12 servings

My Aunt Evelyn is a portable baker. Wherever she goes, there's a cake in tow. If you need a moist chocolate cake to carry along to a picnic, one that will transport easily, right in the pan, this one is it. It is one that you can cut up into squares and eat out of your hand with a napkin instead of a plate and fork.

Cake

2 cups all-purpose flour

2 cups granulated sugar

1 teaspoon baking soda

Pinch of salt

8 tablespoons (1 stick) unsalted butter, cut up

8 tablespoons (1 stick) margarine, cut up

1 cup water

1/3 cup unsweetened cocoa powder
   (not Dutch process)

3/4 cup sour cream

2 large eggs

1 teaspoon vanilla extract

Frosting

8 tablespoons (1 stick) unsalted butter, cut up

1/3 cup plus 1 tablespoon milk

1/4 cup unsweetened cocoa powder
   (not Dutch process)

1 pound about 4 1/3 cups confectioners'
   sugar, sifted

1 teaspoon vanilla extract

1 cup (4 ounces) coarsely chopped
   pecans, toasted

To make the cake, position a rack in the center of the oven and preheat to 350°F. Lightly butter and flour a 13 x 9-inch baking pan, tapping out the excess flour.

Whisk the flour, granulated sugar, baking soda, and salt in a large bowl to combine. In a medium saucepan, bring the butter, margarine, water, and cocoa to a boil over high heat, stirring to dissolve the butter and margarine. Pour into the flour mixture and whisk well. Add the sour cream, then the eggs and vanilla, and beat well. Spread evenly in the pan.

Bake until the cake springs back when pressed in the center, about 35 minutes. Remove from the oven and place on a wire rack.

Meanwhile, make the frosting. Bring the butter, milk, and cocoa to a boil in a large saucepan over medium heat, stirring to dissolve the butter. Gradually stir in the confectioners' sugar, then the vanilla. Stir in the chopped pecans. Pour over the warm cake.

Cool the cake in the pan on the rack. Cut into pieces and serve directly from the pan.

Spring Vegetable Lasagne

Makes 9 servings

This is a perfect one-dish meal to take to a grieving family. It is well-liked by children as well as adults.

Béchamel Sauce

3 cups milk

1 small onion, sliced

2 garlic cloves, crushed under a knife
    and peeled

3 sprigs of fresh thyme or $1/4$ teaspoon
    dried thyme

6 tablespoons ($3/4$ stick) unsalted butter

3 tablespoons all-purpose flour

Lasagne

$1/2$ cup freshly grated Parmesan cheese

Salt and freshly ground black pepper

1 pound asparagus, trimmed and cut in half
    lengthwise if thick

$1 1/2$ pounds (3 medium) Yukon Gold potatoes,
    peeled and cut into $1/4$-inch-thick rounds

9 ounces Fresh Lasagne Noodles (page 164) or
    12 ounces dried lasagne noodles

1 tablespoon extra-virgin olive oil

$1 1/2$ cups (6 ounces) shredded Italian Fontina
    or white Cheddar cheese

4 ounces prosciutto, very thinly sliced

$1/4$ cup freshly grated Parmesan cheese

2 tablespoons unsalted butter, cut into pieces

Chopped fresh parsley, for garnish

To make the béchamel, bring the milk, onion, garlic, and thyme to a simmer in a medium saucepan over medium heat. Remove from the heat and infuse for 10 minutes. Strain, discarding the solids.

Melt the butter in a medium saucepan over medium-low heat. Whisk in the flour and let bubble without browning for 2 minutes. Whisk in the warm milk and bring to a simmer. Cook, whisking often, until the sauce is smooth with no taste of raw flour, about 5 minutes. Remove from the heat and stir in the Parmesan. Season to taste with salt and pepper. Transfer to a bowl. Press a piece of plastic wrap directly onto the surface of the sauce to keep a skin from forming.

Bring a large pot of lightly salted water to a boil over high heat. Add the asparagus and cook until crisp-tender, about 3 minutes. Using a skimmer, transfer the asparagus to a bowl of ice water. Drain and pat dry.

Add the potatoes to the boiling water and cook until almost tender, about 10 minutes. Drain and set aside.

Cook the pasta in boiling salted water, 1 sheet at a time, stirring to keep the sheets separate. Cook until barely tender, about 2 minutes for fresh pasta (follow the package instructions if using dried pasta). Drain and rinse under cold water. Toss the pasta with the oil.

continued on next page

Spring Vegetable Lasagne continued

Position a rack in the center of the oven and preheat to 350°F. Lightly butter a 13 x 9-inch baking dish. Spread a thin film of the béchamel sauce (warm over low heat, if necessary) in the bottom of the dish. Arrange 3 or 4 pasta sheets in the pan, slightly overlapping and trimming as needed. Spread with one third of the sauce, half each of the potatoes, asparagus, Fontina cheese, and prosciutto. Top with another layer of pasta, half of the remaining sauce, and the remaining potatoes, asparagus, Fontina, and prosciutto. Finish with a layer of pasta and spread with the remaining sauce. Sprinkle with the Parmesan cheese and dot with the butter.

Bake until the sauce is bubbling and the top is golden, about 30 minutes. Let stand for 10 minutes before serving. Serve hot, sprinkling each portion with parsley.

Macaroni and Cheese

Makes 6 to 8 servings

Macaroni and cheese is one of those dishes that kids everywhere seem to love – as long as it isn't too fancy. I keep the kids in my life in mind whenever I bake up a dish, and I keep it as mild as possible. When grown-ups are around, you can use more Cheddar cheese or omit the American cheese entirely.

1 pound penne or elbow macaroni

4 tablespoons (1/2 stick) unsalted butter

1/3 cup all-purpose flour

4 cups milk, heated

2 cups (8 ounces) shredded extra-sharp Cheddar cheese

2 cups (8 ounces) finely chopped American cheese

Salt and freshly ground pepper

Hot pepper sauce

1/4 cup (1 ounce) freshly grated Parmesan cheese

Bring a large pot of lightly salted water to a boil over high heat. Add the penne and cook until al dente. Drain well.

Position a rack in the center of the oven and preheat the oven to 350°F. Butter a deep 4-quart casserole.

Melt the butter in a medium saucepan over medium heat. Whisk in the flour. Gradually whisk in the milk. Bring to a simmer, stirring constantly, until the sauce thickens. Reduce the heat to low and simmer for 5 minutes.

Remove from the heat and stir in 1 cup of the Cheddar cheese and 1 cup of the American cheese. Season to taste with salt, pepper, and hot sauce.

Combine the remaining Cheddar and American cheeses. Spread one third of the penne over the bottom of the casserole dish. Top with half of the shredded cheese and a third of the sauce. Repeat, using another third of the penne with the remaining cheese and half of the sauce. Finish with the remaining penne and sauce. Sprinkle Parmesan cheese over the top.

Bake until bubbly and golden brown around the edges, about 30 minutes.

Family Celebrations

Families can throw a party anytime. No need for
a special occasion, although special occasions should
never be overlooked.

Bake a cake or make a pan of fudge to mark a baby's first step, the arrival of a litter of kittens, the winter's first snowfall, or the last day of school. Take a few moments together to celebrate the event. Everyone will leap at the chance to capture a precious memory and have a little party.

All my life I have put myself into situations where there might be a party. These include holidays and birthdays, as well as life's small "non-events," but regardless of the reason, the celebration is always enlivened with food – usually something sweet. We make cakes and candies because they remind us of the sweetness of life, and so I have collected them here for you to pick and choose from for your own family's celebrations.

Candy making is an old-fashioned art that I fear is slipping away. Most of us buy candies, but taking the time to make Peanut Brittle, Buttermilk Pralines, and Pecan Divinity says how much you care. I usually serve homemade candies or little cookies with coffee or tea after dinner parties and try to have them on hand when I have houseguests. Cake baking is more familiar to most folks, but it, too, is considered tricky by some. Nothing could be farther from the truth. I love the expression on people's faces when I present them with a cake. It turns an otherwise minor event into a celebration and leaves us with sweet memories.

Pound cakes are the reigning cakes of the South, perhaps because as a rural region for so many years, eggs, butter, and flour were in every kitchen in good supply. We eat pound cakes all year long, and in the summer it's customary to serve them with sweetened strawberries and whipped cream – the South's version of strawberry shortcake.

My family lives more than a thousand miles from my adopted city of Chicago but on any holiday or special day in the life of our family, I can expect to find a pound cake in my mailbox. This could be from my mother, my Aunt Evelyn, or my Grandmother Mabel, but regardless of who sends it, I know it was mixed, baked, and packaged for mailing with love. The gesture keeps the family connected. And I send similar cakes to loved ones, too – it's an easy task to make my Lemon-Sour Cream Pound Cake, or if I am feeling slightly more ambitious, my Kumquat-Ginger Pound Cake.

Almost everyone makes or buys a cake for a birthday. These days are important. All of us (even those who claim they don't care about birthdays!) would like others to remember two things: our names and our birthdays. My advice after years of being part of a family, observing the families I have worked for, and listening to my created family of friends: Don't believe anyone who says he or she does not want a birthday cake! Everyone wants one.

Where I come from, birthday cakes can be any kind of cake, from a plain pound cake to fancier layer cakes such as my Hummingbird Cake. For a delectable Southern tradition, bake the Coconut Cake with Fluffy Icing. Now that's what I call a cake! My great-grandmother frequently made the Smith Family's Twelve-Layer Chocolate Cake, which I have included in this chapter. She made it with cocoa because that was all she could get; good-quality baking chocolate just was not available in the rural deep South in her time. She baked the layers in cast-iron skillets and each layer was very thin, almost like a pancake. She stacked these and iced them with an icing made with evaporated milk. Not fancy, but we loved it.

Don't fret about making an elaborate cake. Some people believe a birthday cake should be decorated with complicated icing roses, curls, and bows, but the happy truth is a simple cake with a candle stuck in the middle and something as straightforward as "Happy Birthday! We Love You!" written on top provides a message that will resonate for years to come. Even more, perhaps, than if you buy the most intricate and gorgeous bakery-made cake. On the other hand, if you don't have time to bake a cake, a store-bought one still speaks volumes.

Cakes are equally appropriate for holidays, graduations, showers, christenings, Bar Mitzvahs, and anniversaries. If you can name it, you can probably make a cake to celebrate it!

My friends Katrina Markoff and Julie Lang own Vosges Haut-Chocolat, a fabulous chocolate company in Chicago. Katrina told me that when she was a girl, she brought cake to school whether it was anyone's birthday or not. In cahoots with her classmates, she told the teacher it was so-and-so's birthday, and the teacher gladly shortened class time so that the entire class could celebrate by eating the cake. I love this story because it illustrates the power of a cake!

All of us would like others to remember two things: our names and our birthdays.

Coconut Cake with Fluffy Icing

Makes 12 servings

For extra coconut flavor in this cake, I use coconut milk in the batter. If you have the elbow grease, combine the shredded sweetened coconut with shredded fresh coconut. It may sound like using all fresh coconut is a good idea, but I have found that most people prefer a combination of the two, as a cake completely covered with fresh coconut seems a bit too coarse and not sweet enough.

Lemon Filling

$1/3$ cup plus 1 tablespoon fresh lemon juice

$1/4$ cup water

4 teaspoons cornstarch

$3/4$ cup sugar

4 large egg yolks

Grated zest of 2 lemons

4 tablespoons ($1/2$ stick) unsalted butter, cut up

Cake

3 cups cake flour

1 teaspoon baking powder

$1/4$ teaspoon salt

1 cup (2 sticks) unsalted butter, at room temperature

2 cups sugar

4 large eggs, at room temperature, separated (see Note, page 32)

1 teaspoon vanilla extract

1 cup canned coconut milk (not sweetened cream of coconut)

Fluffy Icing

$1 1/2$ cups sugar

2 large egg whites, at room temperature (see Note, page 32)

$1/3$ cup water

2 teaspoons corn syrup

$1/4$ teaspoon cream of tartar

1 teaspoon vanilla extract

One 7-ounce bag shredded sweetened coconut ($2 2/3$ cups) or $1 1/3$ cups shredded sweetened coconut and $1 1/3$ cups fresh shredded coconut (see Note).

To make the filling, combine the lemon juice and water in a heavy-bottomed medium saucepan. Sprinkle with the cornstarch and whisk to dissolve. Stir in the sugar, egg yolks, lemon zest, and butter. Stir constantly over medium-low heat until the mixture comes to a full simmer. Reduce the heat to very low and stir for 1 minute. Strain through a wire sieve into a medium bowl. Press a piece of plastic wrap directly on the surface and cool completely. (The filling can be made 2 days ahead, covered, and refrigerated.)

To make the cake, position a rack in the center of the oven and preheat to 350°F. Lightly butter and flour two 9-inch round cake pans and tap out the excess flour. Line the bottoms of the pans with parchment paper.

Sift together the flour, baking powder, and salt. Using a hand-held electric mixer on high speed, beat the butter and sugar in a large bowl until light and fluffy, about 3 minutes. Beat in the egg yolks, one at a time, then the vanilla. On low speed, add the flour in 3 additions, alternating with 2 additions of the coconut milk, beginning and ending with the flour, and beat until smooth, scraping down the sides of the bowl often with a rubber spatula.

Beat the egg whites in a medium bowl with clean beaters on high speed until they form stiff peaks. Stir one fourth of the whites into the batter, then fold in the remainder. Spread evenly in the pans.

Bake, being sure the pans don't touch each other and that they clear the sides of the oven by 2 inches, until a toothpick inserted in the centers comes out clean, 25 to 30 minutes.

Let cool in the pans on wire racks for 10 minutes. Invert onto the racks and unmold, removing the wax paper. Turn right sides up and cool completely.

To make the icing, combine the sugar, egg whites, water, corn syrup, and cream of tartar in the top of a double boiler. Place over simmering water. Beat on high speed with a hand-held electric mixer until the icing forms stiff, shiny peaks, about 7 minutes. Remove from the heat and beat in the vanilla extract.

Place 1 layer upside down on a serving plate. Spread with the lemon filling. Place the other layer on top, right side up. Spread the icing over the top and then the sides of the cake. Press handfuls of the coconut all over the icing. The cake is best the day it is made.

Note: *Choose a coconut that sounds as if it is full of juice when shaken and with clean "eyes" free of any mold. Place the coconut on a baking sheet and bake in a pre-heated 400°F oven for 15 minutes. Cool slightly. Protecting your hand with a kitchen towel, hold the coconut over the sink and rap with a hammer around the coconut's equator until it cracks. Using a sturdy knife, pry the coconut meat out of the shell. Pare the meat with a vegetable peeler. Shred the coconut in a food processor fitted with a fine shredding blade or on a box grater.*

Love Goddess Cake

Makes 10 to 12 servings

Unique and exotic, this cake is likely to arouse passion in whoever is lucky enough to indulge in a slice. Chocolate, chiles, and vanilla were all found in the jungles of Mexico, and the Aztec rulers combined them to make a drink that they believed had aphrodisiacal properties. It is the invention of two talented Chicagoans, Julie Lang and Katrina Markoff, co-founders of Vosges Haut-Chocolat. At their chocolate shop, they make it in small heart-shaped cakes to feed one or two people, but for home cooks, a larger cake is more practical. You can bake it in regular round cake pans, if you want, and while it may not look as sexy as a small heart shape, it will still be fantastic. (See Sources, *page 278, for heart-shaped cake pans.)*

Cake

Butter, for the pans

1 cup Vosges Haut-Chocolat Aztec Elixir Cocoa (see Note) or unsweetened Dutch-process cocoa powder

1 cup boiling water

1 cup water, at tap temperature

2³⁄₄ cups all-purpose flour

2 teaspoons baking soda

¹⁄₂ teaspoon baking powder

¹⁄₂ teaspoon salt

1 teaspoon pure ground ancho chile powder (see *Sources*, page 278), if not using Aztec Elixir Cocoa (optional)

1 cup (2 sticks) unsalted butter, at room temperature

continued on next page

Love Goddess Cake continued

2¼ cups granulated sugar

4 large eggs, at room temperature (see Note,
  page 32)

2 vanilla beans, preferably Mexican, ground
  in a coffee grinder until very finely chopped,
  or 2 teaspoons vanilla extract

Filling

¼ cup plus 2 tablespoons heavy cream

3½ ounces bittersweet chocolate,
  finely chopped

½ teaspoon pure ground ancho chile powder
  (see *Sources*, page 278)

⅛ teaspoon pure ground chipotle chile powder
  (see *Sources*, page 278), optional

8 tablespoons (1 stick) unsalted butter,
  at room temperature

Frosting

2 cups heavy cream

½ cup confectioners' sugar

1 teaspoon vanilla extract

Pesticide-free, edible flowers, such as
  nasturtiums and roses, for garnish

Position a rack in the center of the oven and pre-heat to 350°F. Lightly butter two 9 x 2-inch heart-shaped cake pans. Line the bottoms of the pans with wax paper. Dust the sides of the pans with flour and tap out the excess.

To make the cake, whisk the cocoa and boiling water in a medium bowl until smooth. Whisk in the water and let stand until the mixture cools.

Sift together the flour, baking soda, baking powder, salt, and chile powder, if using. Beat the butter and sugar in a large bowl with a hand-held electric mixer at high speed until the mixture is light in color and texture, about 3 minutes. Beat in the eggs, one at a time, then the chopped vanilla beans or extract. On low speed, add the flour in 3 additions, alternating with 2 additions of the cocoa mixture, scraping the bowl often, until smooth. Spread the batter evenly in the pans, filling each pan no more than two-thirds full (discard any extra batter or pour into muffin tins to bake as cupcakes).

Bake until a wooden toothpick inserted in the centers of the cakes comes out clean, 25 to 30 minutes. Transfer to a wire rack and cool for 5 minutes. Invert onto the racks, remove the wax paper, and cool completely. (The cake layers can be prepared up to 1 day ahead, wrapped tightly in plastic wrap, and stored at room temperature.)

To make the filling, bring the cream to a simmer in a small saucepan over high heat. Place the chocolate in a medium bowl and pour the hot cream over it. Let stand until the chocolate soft-ens, about 5 minutes, then whisk until smooth. Whisk in the ancho powder and chipotle pow-der, if using. Let stand until completely cooled, about 1 hour.

Using a hand-held electric mixer at medium speed, beat in the butter, 1 tablespoon at a time, until the filling is smooth. Do not overbeat.

To make the frosting, whip the cream, confec-tioners' sugar, and vanilla in a chilled medium bowl with a hand-held electric mixer on high speed just until stiff. Do not overbeat.

Place 1 cake layer, upside down, on a serving platter. Spread with the chocolate filling. Top with the other cake layer, right side up. Spread a thin layer of the frosting over the top and sides of the cake, to seal the dark crumbs onto the cake so they don't mar the white frosting. Now frost the cake with the remaining frosting, slathering it on and trying not to disturb the first coat. Refrigerate, uncovered, until ready to serve. (The cake can be prepared up to 8 hours ahead. If chilled, let the cake stand for about 30 minutes before serving.) Just before serving, decorate with the flowers.

Note: *Vosges Haut-Chocolat Aztec Elixir Cocoa is a combination of cocoa, vanilla, spices, and ground chiles. It is available at some specialty grocers and by mail order (see* Sources, *page 278).*

Lemon-Sour Cream Pound Cake

Makes 12 servings

Sour cream is the secret ingredient in many a pound cake. This one is based on a lemon pound cake from my family's recipe collection.

3 cups all-purpose flour

1/2 teaspoon baking powder

1/4 teaspoon baking soda

1/2 teaspoon salt

1 cup (2 sticks) unsalted butter, at room temperature

3 cups sugar

6 large eggs, at room temperature (see Note, page 32)

1 teaspoon vanilla extract

Grated zest of 2 lemons

1 cup sour cream, at room temperature

Lemon Syrup

Zest of 1 lemon

1 cup fresh lemon juice

1/4 cup water

2/3 cup sugar

To make the cake, position a rack in the center of the oven and preheat to 325°F. Butter and flour a 10-inch fluted tube (Bundt) pan, and tap out the excess flour.

Sift the flour, baking powder, baking soda, and salt together; set aside. Beat the butter and sugar in a large bowl with a hand-held electric mixer on high speed until light and fluffy, about 3 minutes. Beat in the eggs, one at a time, then the vanilla and zest. On low speed, add the flour in 3 additions, alternating with 2 additions of the sour cream, beginning and ending with the flour, and beat until smooth, scraping down the sides of the bowl often with a rubber spatula. Spread evenly in the pan.

Bake until a wooden skewer inserted in the center of the cake comes out clean, about 1 1/4 hours.

Meanwhile, make the syrup. Bring the lemon juice, zest, water, and sugar, to a boil over high heat and cook until it is reduced to 1/2 cup, about 15 minutes. Allow syrup to cool before drizzling onto the cake.

Transfer the cake to a wire rack and cool for 10 minutes. Drizzle half of the syrup over the cake. Invert onto the rack and brush with the remaining syrup. Cool completely.

Hummingbird Cake

Makes 12 servings

This wonderful cake was an inspiration from my childhood friend Susan Turner, an amazing baker. In later years it has become my trademark, as it was hers in Tallahassee, and now will become yours.

Cake

3 cups all-purpose flour

2 cups granulated sugar

1 teaspoon baking soda

1 teaspoon ground cinnamon

$1/2$ teaspoon salt

2 cups chopped ripe bananas

1 cup drained crushed pineapple

1 cup vegetable oil, preferably canola

3 large eggs, beaten

$1^1/2$ teaspoons vanilla extract

1 cup (4 ounces) finely chopped pecans

Icing

8 ounces cream cheese, at room temperature

$1/2$ cup (1 stick) butter, at room temperature

1 pound confectioners' sugar (about $4^1/2$ cups), sifted

1 teaspoon vanilla extract

Pesticide-free, edible flowers from the garden, such as roses, nasturtiums, or pansies, for garnish (optional)

To make the cake, position racks in the center and bottom third of the oven and preheat to 350°F. Lightly butter two 9-inch round cake pans, sprinkle evenly with flour, and tap out the excess. (If you wish, butter the pans, line the bottoms with rounds of parchment paper, then flour the pans and tap out the excess.)

Sift the flour, sugar, baking soda, cinnamon, and salt into a bowl. In another bowl, stir or whisk the bananas, pineapple, oil, eggs, and vanilla, until combined. Do not use an electric mixer. Pour into the dry mixture and fold together with a large spatula just until smooth. Do not beat. Fold in the pecans. Spread evenly in the pans.

Bake until the cakes spring back when pressed in the center, 30 to 35 minutes. Transfer the cakes to wire racks and cool for 10 minutes. Invert the cakes onto the racks (remove the parchment paper now, if using). Turn right side up and cool completely.

To make the icing, using an electric mixer on high speed, beat the cream cheese and butter in a large bowl until combined. On low speed, gradually beat in the sugar, then the vanilla, to make a smooth icing.

Place 1 cake layer, upside down, on a serving platter. Spread with about $2/3$ cup of the icing. Top with the second layer, right side up. Spread the remaining icing over the top and sides of the cake. (The cake can be prepared up to 1 day ahead and stored, uncovered, in the refrigerator. Let stand at room temperature for 1 hour before serving.) Just before serving, decorate the top with the flowers, if desired.

Red Velvet Cake with Chocolate Frosting

Makes 12 servings

A chocolate cake with a light, velvety crumb, it gets its red color from the unashamed use of red food coloring (my original recipe used an entire one-ounce bottle, which was just a bit too shocking). Pour yourself a glass of milk and pull up to a slice of this chocolate beauty.

Cake

2¹/2 cups cake flour (not self-rising)

3 tablespoons cocoa powder (not Dutch process)

1 teaspoon baking soda

1 teaspoon salt

1 cup buttermilk

1 teaspoon red food coloring

1 teaspoon vanilla extract

1 teaspoon distilled white vinegar

8 tablespoons (1 stick) unsalted butter, at room temperature

1¹/2 cups granulated sugar

2 large eggs, at room temperature (see Note, page 32)

Frosting

4 ounces bittersweet chocolate, finely chopped

1 pound (about 4¹/3 cups) confectioners' sugar

3 tablespoons unsweetened cocoa powder

8 tablespoons (1 stick) unsalted butter

1 teaspoon vanilla extract

¹/3 cup cooled brewed coffee, as needed

Position a rack in the center of the oven, and preheat to 350°F. Butter two 9-inch layer pans. Line the bottoms of the pans with parchment paper. Dust with flour and tap out the excess.

To make the cake, sift the flour, cocoa, baking soda, and salt together. Mix the buttermilk, food coloring, vanilla, and vinegar in a glass measuring cup. Beat the butter and sugar in a large bowl with a hand-held electric mixer on high speed until light and fluffy, about 3 minutes. Beat in the eggs, one at a time. On low speed, add the flour in 3 additions, alternating with 2 additions of the buttermilk, beginning and ending with the flour, and beat until smooth, scraping down the sides of the bowl often with a rubber spatula. Spread evenly in the pans.

Bake until a wooden toothpick inserted in the centers of the cakes comes out clean, 25 to 30 minutes.

Transfer the cakes to wire racks and cool for 10 minutes. Invert onto the racks and remove the parchment paper. Turn right side up and cool completely.

To make the frosting, melt the chocolate in the top part of a double boiler over very hot but not simmering water. Remove from the heat and cool until tepid.

Sift together the confectioners' sugar and cocoa. Beat the butter in a large bowl with a hand-held electric mixer on medium speed until creamy. On low speed, gradually beat in the sugar-cocoa mixture. Beat in the cooled chocolate, then the vanilla. Gradually beat in enough of the coffee to make a smooth frosting.

Place 1 cake layer upside down on the serving plate and frost with about 1/2 cup of the frosting. Top with the second layer, right side up. Frost the top and then the sides with the remaining frosting. (The cake can be made 1 day ahead and refrigerated, uncovered. Bring to room temperature before serving.)

Tropical Upside-Down Cake

Makes 12 servings

Upside-down cake is an American classic. My variation uses mangoes and pineapple. Enjoy!

12 tablespoons (1 1/2 sticks) unsalted butter,
    at room temperature

1 1/2 cups pitted, peeled, and (1-inch) cubed ripe
    mango (about 2 mangoes)

1 1/2 cups peeled, cored, and (1-inch) cubed ripe
    pineapple (about 1/2 small pineapple)

1 cup (packed) light brown sugar

2 tablespoons dark rum

2 cups cake flour

2 teaspoons baking powder

1 teaspoon ground ginger

Pinch of salt

1 cup granulated sugar

2 large eggs, at room temperature (see Note,
    page 32)

1 teaspoon vanilla extract

3/4 cup milk

1/2 cup (2 ounces) coarsely chopped
    pecans, toasted

Vanilla ice cream, for serving

Position a rack in the center of the oven and preheat to 350°F. Generously butter a 13 x 9-inch baking pan.

Heat 4 tablespoons of the butter in a large skillet over medium heat. Add the mango, pineapple, brown sugar, and rum. Cook, stirring often, until the sugar is melted and bubbling. Cool until tepid.

Sift together the flour, baking powder, ginger, and salt and set aside. Beat the remaining 8 tablespoons of butter and the sugar in a large bowl with a hand-held electric mixer at high speed until light and fluffy, about 3 minutes. Beat in the eggs, one at a time, then the vanilla. On low speed, add the flour in 3 additions, alternating with 2 additions of the milk, and beat until smooth, scraping down the sides of the bowl often with a rubber spatula.

Arrange the fruit in a single layer in the pan, and pour the syrup over all. Sprinkle with the pecans. Spread the batter evenly over the fruit.

Bake until a toothpick inserted in the center of the cake comes out clean, about 35 minutes. Cool for 10 minutes on a wire rack. Invert and unmold onto a large serving platter. (If any pieces of fruit stay in the pan, just remove them and arrange them in their place on the cake.) Pour any juices in the pan over the cake. Serve warm or completely cooled, with the ice cream.

Triple-Layer German Chocolate Cake

Makes 12 servings

Surprising as it may seem, this recipe has nothing to do with Germany. A Mr. German developed a sweet choco-late for the Baker chocolate company, but the brand didn't take off until German's chocolate cake recipe was published in a Texas newspaper. Proving that there is never too much of a good thing, my recipe makes a tall, triple-layer tower of chocolate heaven, with lots of the classic coconut-pecan frosting.

Cake

6 ounces German's Sweet Chocolate,
   finely chopped

1/2 cup boiling water

3 cups cake flour

1 teaspoon baking soda

Pinch of salt

1 cup (2 sticks) unsalted butter, at room
   temperature

2 cups sugar

4 large eggs, at room temperature
   (see Note, page 32)

1 teaspoon vanilla extract

1 cup buttermilk

1/2 cup sweetened shredded coconut

Frosting

1 cup evaporated milk

1 cup sugar

8 tablespoons (1 stick) unsalted butter, cut up

2 large eggs

2 cups sweetened shredded coconut

1 cup (4 ounces) coarsely chopped
   pecans, toasted

1 teaspoon vanilla extract

To make the cake, position a rack in the center of the oven and preheat to 350°F. Lightly butter and flour three 9-inch round cake pans and tap out the excess flour. Line the bottoms of the pans with parchment paper.

Place the chocolate in a small bowl and pour the boiling water over it. Let stand 3 minutes to soften the chocolate, then whisk until smooth. Cool.

Sift together the flour, baking soda, and salt. Using a hand-held electric mixer on high speed, beat the butter and sugar in a large bowl until light and fluffy, about 3 minutes. Beat in the eggs, one at a time, then the vanilla. Beat in the chocolate. On low speed, add the flour in 3 additions, alternating with 2 additions of the buttermilk, beginning and ending with the flour, and beat until smooth, scraping down the sides of the bowl often with a rubber spatula. Mix in the coconut. Spread evenly in the pans.

continued on next page

Triple-Layer German Chocolate Cake continued

Bake, being sure the pans don't touch each other and that they clear the sides of the oven by 2 inches, until a toothpick inserted in the centers comes out clean, about 30 minutes.

Let cool in the pans on wire racks for 10 minutes. Invert onto the racks and unmold. Remove the parchment paper. Turn right side up and cool completely.

To make the frosting, whisk the evaporated milk, sugar, butter, and eggs in a medium saucepan until combined. Cook over medium-low heat, stirring constantly with a wooden spoon, until the mixture is caramel colored and thick enough to coat the spoon, about 12 minutes. The mixture should not come to a boil. Remove from the heat and stir in the coconut, pecans, and vanilla. Let stand, stirring often, until cool and thick enough to spread.

If desired, trim the tops of the cakes to level the layers. Stack the layers on a serving plate, spreading the top of each with the frosting, and leaving the sides unfrosted.

The Smith Family's Twelve-Layer Cake

Makes 16 to 20 servings

A recipe from my great-great-grandmother, this cake has taken center stage at many Smith family celebrations. It is a stack of twelve thin yellow-cake layers that are held together with a cocoa icing that is just this side of a syrup. If you buy a dozen inexpensive aluminum-foil cake pans (they can be saved for another time), you will be able to knock out the layers in no time.

Cake Layers

4 1/2 cups all-purpose flour, sifted

1 1/2 teaspoons baking powder

1/4 teaspoon salt

1 1/2 cups (3 sticks) unsalted butter, at room temperature

2 1/2 cups sugar

6 large eggs, at room temperature (see Note, page 32)

3 cups milk

1 1/2 teaspoons vanilla extract

Icing

3 cups sugar

1/2 cup unsweetened cocoa powder, preferably Dutch process

1 cup (2 sticks) unsalted butter, cut up

One 12-ounce can evaporated milk

1 tablespoon vanilla extract

Pecan halves, for garnish

Position racks in the center and bottom third of the oven and preheat to 375°F. Lightly butter four 8½- to 9-inch cake pans (you will bake the cakes in 3 batches) and line the bottoms with rounds of parchment paper. Flour the pans and tap out the excess.

To make the layers, sift together the sifted flour, baking powder, and salt. Sift the mixture one more time, and set aside.

Beat the butter and sugar in the bowl of a heavy-duty electric mixer fitted with the paddle blade on high speed until light in color and texture, about 3 minutes. Beat in the eggs, one at a time. Scrape down the bowl and be sure the mixture is well blended. On low speed, add the flour in 3 additions, alternating with 2 additions of the milk, beginning and ending with the flour, and beat until smooth, scraping down the sides of the bowl often with a rubber spatula. Beat in the vanilla. Using a scant cup for each layer, spread the batter evenly in the pans. It will make a thin layer.

Staggering the pans on the racks so they are at least 2 inches from each other and the sides of the oven and not directly over each other, bake the layers until they feel firm when pressed in the centers and are beginning to pull away from the sides of the pans, about 12 minutes. Cool in the pans for 5 minutes. Invert the layers onto cake racks, remove the parchment paper, and cool completely. Wash and prepare the pans. Repeat the procedure until all 12 layers have been baked and cooled.

To make the icing, bring the sugar, cocoa, butter, and evaporated milk to a full boil in a large saucepan. Reduce the heat to medium-low and cook until the icing has thickened slightly (it will resemble chocolate syrup but will thicken as it cools), about 3 minutes. Stir in the vanilla. Let the icing cool until thick enough to spread, but still pourable.

Place a layer of cake on a wire rack set over a jelly-roll pan. Spread with a few tablespoons of the icing, letting the excess run down the sides. Stack the remaining cakes, icing each layer. Pour the remaining icing over the top of the cake. If you wish, smooth the icing on the edges to cover the sides. Place pecan halves around the top perimeter of the cake. Let stand until the glaze sets. (The cake is best served the day it is made. To store, cover loosely with plastic wrap and refrigerate for up to 1 day.)

Kumquat-Ginger Pound Cake

Makes 12 servings

This special recipe is based on my family's pound cake recipe, but with an exotic twist. Kumquats, which are members of the citrus family and which look like tiny elongated oranges, have a perfume-like aroma and tart flavor. They should be used by more cooks during their season in late fall and early winter! Kumquats are usually eaten peel and all, and that peel adds extra flavor to baked goods. I originally created this as a birthday cake for my friend Margie Geddes, on the motor yacht Mrs. Red Stripe, *with local kumquats during a boat trip in Florida's west coast islands. It has been a favorite ever since. For a real treat, serve it with a cup of hot ginger green tea.*

Cake

3 cups all-purpose flour

1 teaspoon baking powder

¼ teaspoon salt

1 cup (2 sticks) unsalted butter, at room temperature

2 cups sugar

5 large eggs, at room temperature (see Note, page 32)

1 cup whole milk

¼ cup finely chopped kumquats

1 teaspoon vanilla extract

Glaze

1 cup sugar

1 cup fresh orange juice

10 kumquats, thinly sliced

2 tablespoons thinly slivered peeled ginger

To make the cake, position a rack in the center of the oven and preheat to 325°F. Butter and flour a 10-inch fluted tube (Bundt) pan, tapping out the excess flour.

Sift the flour, baking powder, and salt. Using an electric mixer on high speed, beat the butter and sugar in a large bowl until very light and fluffy, about 3 minutes. Beat in the eggs one at a time. On low speed, add the flour in 3 additions, alternating with 2 additions of the milk, beginning and ending with the flour, and beat until smooth, scraping down the sides of the bowl often with a rubber spatula. Beat in the chopped kumquats and vanilla. Spread evenly in the prepared pan.

Bake until a wooden skewer inserted in the center of the cake comes out clean, about 1 hour and 15 minutes. Cool on a wire rack for 10 minutes.

Meanwhile, make the glaze. Bring the sugar, orange juice, sliced kumquats, and ginger to a boil over high heat, stirring to dissolve the sugar. Reduce the heat to low and simmer until the kumquats are translucent and the liquid is syrupy, about 15 minutes. Strain through a wire sieve, reserving the kumquats and ginger.

Drizzle half of the glaze over the warm cake. Invert onto a wire rack placed over a jelly-roll pan. Brush the cake with the remaining glaze. Arrange the candied kumquats and ginger over the top of the cake. (The cake can be prepared 3 days ahead, covered with plastic wrap, and stored at room temperature. Or wrap it in plastic wrap and aluminum foil, then freeze for up to 3 months.)

Buttermilk Pralines

Makes about twenty-four 3-inch pralines

Pralines are probably the ultimate Southern sweet. Unlike other candies that are problematic to make under humid conditions, pralines aren't temperamental. This buttermilk version makes them especially creamy.

3 cups (packed) light brown sugar

1 cup buttermilk

1/4 teaspoon cream of tartar

4 tablespoons (1/2 stick) unsalted butter, plus
softened butter for the parchment paper

3 cups (12 ounces) pecan halves or pieces

1 teaspoon vanilla extract

Cover an area about 3 x 2-feet on your work surface with parchment paper. Butter the parchment paper with softened butter or spray with nonstick cooking oil.

In a heavy-bottomed large saucepan, bring the brown sugar, buttermilk, and cream of tartar to a boil over high heat, stirring to help dissolve the sugar. Boil, stirring constantly, until a candy thermometer reads 236°F (soft-ball stage).

Remove from the heat and stir in the butter, pecans, and vanilla. Stir until the mixture thickens slightly and begins to lose its gloss but is still pourable. Use a tablespoon to dollop patties of the syrup onto the parchment paper – the pralines should spread and be about 3 inches across. (Use a teaspoon to make them smaller, if you wish.) Cool completely. (The pralines can be made up to 1 week ahead and stored in an airtight container at room temperature.)

Pecan Divinity

Makes about 1 pound

Fluffy white divinity (think of it as vanilla fudge) has graced many candy dishes over the years. Make divinity on a dry, cloudless day to ensure success – humidity can wreak havoc on the candy's texture.

2 1/4 cups sugar

1/2 cup light corn syrup

1/2 cup water

1/4 teaspoon salt

2 large egg whites

1 1/2 teaspoon vanilla extract

1/2 cup coarsely chopped pecans or walnuts

Lightly butter an 8-inch square baking dish. Bring the sugar, corn syrup, water, and salt to a boil in a heavy-bottomed medium casserole over high heat, stirring just until the sugar dissolves. Boil, without stirring, until the syrup reaches 260°F (hard-ball stage) on a candy thermometer.

Just before the syrup reaches 260°F, beat the egg whites in a medium bowl with a hand-held electric mixer on high speed until stiff peaks form. In a slow steady stream, beat the syrup into the whites. Beat in the vanilla. Continue beating until the mixture is very thick and holds its shape, about 6 minutes. Mix in the nuts.

Spread evenly in the baking dish. Cool completely.

Invert the divinity to unmold and cut into squares. (The divinity can be made up to 1 week ahead and stored in an airtight container at room temperature.)

A simple cake with a candle stuck in the middle and something as straightforward as "Happy

Birthday! We Love You!" written on top provides a message that will resonate for years to come.

Peanut Brittle

Makes 1 pound, 2 ounces

Peanut brittle is an old-fashioned treat that deserves to be made at home more often. Don't restrict yourself to peanuts – just about any lightly salted nut will be delicious.

1 cup sugar

$1/2$ cup water

$1/2$ cup light corn syrup

8 ounces lightly salted Spanish peanuts

2 teaspoons unsalted butter

1 teaspoon vanilla extract

1 teaspoon baking soda

Lightly butter a cookie sheet. Bring the sugar, water, and corn syrup to a boil in a heavy-bottomed saucepan over medium-high heat, stirring just until the sugar dissolves.

Cook without stirring until the syrup is golden brown (you won't need a candy thermometer, but if you want to use one, it should read 325°F, or hard-crack stage), 10 to 12 minutes. Remove from the heat.

Stir in the peanuts, butter, vanilla, and baking soda. Pour onto the cookie sheet and pull the brittle to the edges with 2 forks. Be careful, brittle is very hot. Cool completely. Break into pieces. (The peanut brittle can be prepared up to 2 weeks ahead and stored in an airtight container at room temperature.)

Five Pounds of Fudge

Makes 5 pounds

When I was a child, my favorite place to hang out in Jasper, Florida, was at Mrs. Mary Clay's. There on the shelf stood a tin of this most delicious decadent fudge. This recipe is great for someone who wants to give a sweet holiday gift or for someone who has been asked to provide something to sell at a church or school bake sale.

$4^1/2$ cups sugar

1 cup (2 sticks) unsalted butter

1 cup evaporated milk

Two 12-ounce packages semisweet
   chocolate chips

Two $7^1/2$-ounce jars marshmallow cream

1 cup coarsely chopped walnuts

2 ounces unsweetened chocolate,
   finely chopped

Lightly grease a 13 x 9-inch baking pan. Bring the sugar, butter, and evaporated milk to a boil in a large, heavy-bottomed saucepan over medium-high heat, stirring just until the sugar dissolves. Cook, stirring constantly, until a candy thermometer reads 234° to 240°F, or soft-ball stage, about 5 minutes. Remove from the heat.

Add the chocolate chips, marshmallow cream, walnuts, and unsweetened chocolate and stir until the chocolate is melted and the mixture is well combined. Spread evenly in the prepared pan. Cool completely. To serve, cut into squares. (The fudge can be prepared up to 2 weeks ahead and stored in an airtight container at room temperature.)

Pecan Shortbread Cookies

Makes about 2 dozen cookies

Here's an example of what are sometimes called "icebox cookies," because they must be chilled in the refrigerator until firm enough to slice. They could also be called "freezer cookies," because the dough can be frozen for up to two months, then defrosted and sliced. This recipe makes a modest amount of cookies, but the dough is easily doubled or even tripled to make more.

1 cup all-purpose flour

Pinch of ground cinnamon

Pinch of salt

8 tablespoons (1 stick) unsalted butter,
   at room temperature

1/4 cup sugar

1/2 teaspoon vanilla extract

1/2 cup (2 ounces) coarsely chopped
   pecans, toasted

Sift together the flour, cinnamon, and salt and set aside. Beat the butter, sugar, and vanilla in a large bowl with a hand-held electric mixer at high speed until light and fluffy, about 3 minutes. Stir in the flour, then the pecans, to make a stiff dough.

On a lightly floured work surface, form the dough into a 9-inch-long log. Wrap tightly in parchment paper. Refrigerate until chilled and firm, at least 2 hours or overnight.

Position a rack in the center of the oven and preheat to 350°F.

Unwrap and slice the dough into 3/8-inch-thick rounds. Arrange about 1 inch apart on an ungreased baking sheet. Bake until beginning to brown around the edges, about 20 minutes. Cool on the sheet for 5 minutes, then transfer to wire racks to cool completely. (The cookies can be prepared up to 5 days ahead and stored in an airtight container at room temperature.)

Thin Sugar Cookies

Makes about 3 dozen 3-inch cookies

Fredda Hyman sent me this recipe for her family's sugar cookies. I know that every family has a recipe for a favorite cookie – that is exactly why these are so special! Fredda says, "I first became aware of these cookies when I was about eight. Grandma was rolling out the dough with Mom. They looked so serious as they concentrated on rolling out the dough as thinly as possible – important for the cookies to be properly delicate. Eventually, the cookie-making duties passed on to me, and now I am teaching my granddaughters how to make them. No matter how many I make, my sons devour them in one sitting. Remember, when you roll out these cookies, think thin!"

1 1/2 cups all-purpose flour

1/4 teaspoon baking powder

1/2 teaspoon salt

8 tablespoons (1 stick) unsalted butter,
   at room temperature

1 cup sugar

1 large egg, at room temperature (see Note,
   page 32)

1 teaspoon vanilla extract

continued on next page

Thin Sugar Cookies continued

Topping

1/4 cup coarsely chopped walnuts

1/3 cup sugar

1/4 teaspoon ground cinnamon

Candied cherries, cut into small dice (optional)

Whisk the flour, baking powder, and salt in a medium bowl to combine. Beat the butter and sugar in another bowl with a hand-held electric mixer on high speed until the mixture is light in color and texture, about 3 minutes. Beat in the egg and vanilla. On low speed, gradually mix in the flour. Gather up the dough, press into 2 thick disks, and wrap in plastic wrap. Refrigerate until the dough is chilled, at least 1 hour or overnight. (If the dough is chilled until hard, let stand for 10 minutes at room temperature, or it will crack when rolled out.)

Position racks in the center and top third of the oven and preheat to 350°F.

To make the topping, pulse the walnuts, sugar, and cinnamon until the walnuts are very finely chopped. Set aside.

Place 1 disk of dough on a lightly floured work surface and dust the top with flour. Roll out 1/8 inch thick or slightly thinner if you can manage it. Cut out the cookies and place 1 inch apart on ungreased cookie sheets. Sprinkle the nut-sugar on the cookies, trying not to get sugar on the cookie sheets. If desired, decorate the cookies with the candied cherries.

Bake, switching the positions of the sheets from top to bottom and front to back halfway during baking, until the cookies are golden around the edges, 12 to 15 minutes. Let cool for a few minutes on the baking sheets, then transfer to wire racks and cool completely. (The cookies can be stored up to 5 days at room temperature in an airtight container.)

Chocolate, Cherry, and Chile Biscotti

Makes about 28 biscotti

Believe me – give these deliciously spicy cookies a try and expand your palate a bit. Chocolate and chiles are old friends, and the cherries add sweet contrast. Candidates for dipping include full-bodied wines like Zinfandel and Cabernet Sauvignon, port, and espresso.

8 tablespoons (1 stick) unsalted butter, at room temperature

1 cup sugar

Grated zest of 1 large orange

2 large eggs

1 teaspoon vanilla extract

2 cups plus 3 tablespoons all-purpose flour

1 teaspoon baking powder

2 teaspoons pure ground ancho chile powder (see *Sources*, page 278)

1/4 teaspoon salt

3 1/2 ounces coarsely chopped semisweet or bittersweet chocolate

1/2 cup (2 ounces) coarsely chopped walnuts

1/2 cup (3 ounces) dried cherries

Position the racks in the top third and center of the oven and preheat to 350° F.

Using a hand-held electric mixer set at high speed, beat the butter, sugar, and orange zest in a large bowl until well combined, about 3 minutes. Beat in the eggs, one at a time, then the vanilla.

In a medium bowl, whisk the flour, baking powder, chile powder, and salt to combine. Using a wooden spoon, gradually beat in the butter mixture. Work in the chocolate, walnuts, and cherries.

Divide the dough in half. Using lightly floured hands on a floured work surface, form the dough into two 10 x 2-inch logs. Place the logs on an ungreased large baking sheet, at least 2 inches apart. Bake on the center rack until set and golden brown, about 30 minutes. Remove from the oven and let cool on the baking sheet for 20 minutes.

Using a serrated knife and a sawing motion, carefully cut the logs into diagonal slices about 1/2 inch wide. Place the slices on ungreased baking sheets. Bake until the undersides of the biscotti are beginning to brown at the edges, about 8 minutes. Turn the biscotti over. Switch the positions of the baking sheets from top to bottom and front to back. Continue baking until lightly browned on the other side, about 8 minutes more. Cool completely on baking sheets. (The biscotti can be prepared up to 1 week ahead, cooled, and tightly covered in an airtight container at room temperature.)

Gumdrop Cookies

Makes about 4 dozen cookies

My grandmother Mabel always had these in her pantry for us kids to savor. I love their spicy chewy texture.

2 cups sifted all-purpose flour

1 teaspoon baking powder

1 teaspoon baking soda

1/4 teaspoon salt

1 cup vegetable shortening

1 cup (packed) light brown sugar

1 cup granulated sugar

2 large eggs

1 teaspoon vanilla extract

2 cups quick-cooking oats

1 cup sweetened flaked coconut

1 cup (4 ounces) chopped pecans

1 cup spice- or fruit-flavored gumdrops, snipped in half with oiled scissors

Position a rack in the lower third of the oven and preheat to 350°F. Lightly grease 2 large cookie sheets.

Sift together the flour, baking powder, baking soda, and salt. Beat the shortening and brown and granulated sugars in a large bowl with a hand-held electric mixer at high speed until light in color and texture, about 3 minutes. Beat in the eggs, one at a time, blending well after each addition. Blend in the vanilla. With the mixer on low speed, blend in the flour. Stir in the oatmeal, coconut, pecans, and gumdrops with a large, heavy spoon.

continued on next page

Gumdrop Cookies continued

Scoop rounded tablespoons of dough and roll into balls. Place 1 inch apart on the cookie sheets. Flatten each ball slightly with the tines of a fork. Bake until the cookies are lightly browned, about 15 minutes. Transfer to wire racks and cool completely. (The cookies can be prepared up to 1 week ahead and stored in airtight containers at room temperature.)

Lemon Tea Cakes

Makes about 2 dozen cookies

Tender, melt-in-your-mouth cookies that call out for a hot cup of tea.

2 1/2 cups all-purpose flour

2 teaspoons baking powder

Pinch of salt

8 tablespoons (1 stick) unsalted butter,
  at room temperature

1 1/3 cups sugar

2 large eggs, at room temperature

1 teaspoon lemon extract

Grated zest of 1 lemon

1/4 cup evaporated milk

Position racks in the center and top third of the oven and preheat to 375°

Sift together the flour, baking powder, and salt and set aside. Beat the butter and 1 cup of the sugar in a large bowl with a hand-held electric mixer on high speed until light and fluffy, about 3 minutes. Beat in the eggs, one at a time, then the lemon extract and lemon zest. Stir in about 1 cup of the flour, then half of the evaporated milk. Repeat with another cup of flour, the remaining milk, then the remaining flour. If the dough seems soft, cover and refrigerate to firm slightly.

Place the remaining 1/3 cup of sugar in a small bowl. Using about 1 tablespoon of dough for each cookie, roll the dough into balls. Dip each ball into sugar and place it, sugar side up, about 2 inches apart on ungreased baking sheets. Using the bottom of a glass, slightly flatten each ball.

Bake, switching the positions of the sheets from top to bottom and front to back halfway through baking, until the cookies are lightly browned, about 15 minutes. Cool for a few minutes on the sheets, then transfer to wire racks to cool completely. (The cookies can be prepared up to 5 days ahead and stored in an airtight container at room temperature.)

We make cakes and candies because they remind us of the sweetness of life.

Everyone will leap at the chance to capture a precious memory and have a party.

Friends as Family

For many of us, family is the friends who surround us. There are many reasons why our friends naturally become our family over time, but for whatever reason, they are very near and dear to our hearts.

They are the ones who lend an ear and show us love. These bonds are special and unique since we choose to have these people in our lives.

Since I moved from a small town to a big city, I have come to appreciate and value my new family more every year, without ever forsaking my "real family" back home in Florida. I don't believe certain people enter your life by accident. As my mother has told me since I was a little boy, "Darlin', there is a reason for all that happens in your life. When it says hello, say hello back!"

I greet my new family daily and seize every opportunity to sit down and share a meal with them. This is one of the best ways I know to connect with others.

Not too many People have ventured from the tiny town of Jasper in northern Florida to live in a big city. When I decided, after finishing college and then working in Tallahassee for several years, to make Chicago my home, my mother was clearly sad. As much as she agreed that an incredible new world was opening up for me, she still packed endless pairs of thermal underwear in my bags, convinced I needed them to protect me against the cold Midwestern winter. (As it turned out, Mom was right!)

No matter how far I stray, Jasper will always be home; but for now Chicago has offered me a wealth of opportunities to grow and learn about the world. At times, this small-town boy has felt like fleeing the city and running back to Florida, overcome with homesickness and feeling adrift. But I remember my mother's advice, "Chin Up!" and I get through difficult times, often with the help of my new family.

Chicago may be a long way from the green pastures of the Florida farm where I spent so much of my youth, but the fertile Midwest is dotted with small farms that remind me of my roots. Even more immediate are the impressive farmers' markets in the city with offerings that help me remember what home tastes like. July's fresh, juicy peaches and golden corn, August's sweet, vine-ripened tomatoes, and September's crisp apples conspire to take me home whenever I need to feel close to those I left behind.

My new family of friends is one to celebrate. These cherished people come from all walks of life, and many are very different from my Florida family; but all are kindred spirits with whom I enjoy spending time. Making a new friend is a remarkable experience – a meeting of the minds. We all meet hundreds of people in life, but it takes a certain spark to know someone will become a friend. My first friends were all connected to my business and while a few of these wonderful people are still part of my family, I have since acquired friends from other areas of life too.

Like the best of families, a created family allows you to be you. The real you is always the best you; there is no pretense. With our true friends and family, we can be true to ourselves. What a gift that is!

My mother will always be my most treasured confidant, but my new family is also there for me, and I for them. One way we show our connection to each other is by gathering for one of my now-famous Florida country covered-dish suppers.

I invite my friends to bring whatever dish they like, with only a suggestion of specific courses so that we don't end up with nothing but pasta casseroles and cakes. The one course I pay little attention to is what most people think of as hors d'oeuvres. I don't think these fussy little dishes are friendly, and I despise eating while standing up.

The covered dishes might include a family favorite or a new recipe that caught some-one's fancy. I am equally happy to see a person who brings take-out from the deli. He may not have had time to cook, or perhaps he doesn't really enjoy it; but I would much rather he come and join in the conversation than stay home! My Chicago family loves these get-togethers, and the conversation is always filled with laughter and comfortable familiarity.

My first apartment was a cozy little wood-paneled place with a large fireplace and expansive mantle. There was no room for a table, so we set our dishes on the mantle and served ourselves in front of the blazing fire, which was very welcome on frigid Chicago evenings. More often than not, my contribution was Red Beans and Brown Rice, a full-flavored one-dish meal that is as Southern as I am. It's delicious with all sorts of salads, especially Seven-Layer Salad, and Boarding House Biscuits. These are not high-standing biscuits, like the Fluffy Yeast Biscuits; they are almost flat, crunchy on the outside, and fluffy and moist on the inside. These are the biscuits I remember eating as a child. My grandmother sometimes made them with a little bacon grease. Admittedly, it tasted good but I don't use it nowadays. Our covered-dish meal is great when finished with a flaky fruit pie or cobbler, like the Pear and Cranberry Cobbler.

Today I live in a vintage apartment high above Lake Michigan and there's ample space for a dining room table. This makes our covered-dish suppers more manageable, but I confess to missing the fireplace. What I never have to miss is my family. My friends arrive bearing their contributions and looking forward to an enriching meal shared with those we all love.

Here are some selected menu ideas, created from foods in this book. These can help you plan a perfect covered-dish supper or fireplace supper. As you share the meal, the warmth of the love felt by your family will be just as radiant as the fireplace.

So get "Back to the Table" and celebrate family, friends, food, and life's blessings!

Fireplace Supper Menus

Covered Dish Supper Menus

1. Sliced Tomatoes with Fresh Basil

   Spring Vegetable Lasagne, 230

   Fennel, Watercress, and Orange Salad with
      Citrus Vinaigrette, 112

   Focaccia with Roasted Tomatoes and Onion, 73

   Vanilla Citrus Punch, 40

   Chocolate, Cherry, and Chile Biscotti, 260

2. Seeded Cheddar Cheese Straws, 24

   Zucchini, Potato, and Parmesan Soup, 106

   Roast Chicken with Fresh Herbs, 180

   Mixed Herbs and Baby Lettuces with
      Balsamic Vinaigrette, 115

   Peach Buckle, 212

   Iced Tea

   Thin Sugar Cookies, 258

3. Stuffed Eggplant and Roasted
      Tomato Sauce, 143

   Fettuccine with Roasted Asparagus and
      Mushrooms, 146

   Bibb Lettuce Salad with Pecans, Blue Cheese,
      and Pears, 114

   No-Knead Dinner Rolls, 76

   Creamy Custard Pie, 207

   Mineral Water with Lemon

   Pecan Shortbread Cookies, 258

"Family of friends, family of mine, family of yours, family of ours.
Family of families, it is what it is... the family of humankind.

The family of all kinds, family of love. A big family we are.
The blessed family of god."

– Susej

Hyperion, especially

Bob Miller
Will Schwalbe
Linda Prather
Mark Chait
Kiera Hepford

Support Staff

Rick Rodgers – Recipe Tester
Mary Goodbody – Writer
Susan Derecskey – Copy Editor

Dupree Miller Agency

Jan Miller – Book Agent
Michael Broussard – Book Agent
Shannon Marven – Office Manager
Kim Elizondo – Assistant to Jan Miller
Karla Speed – Publicity

Locations

Keith Rudman, The Windsor Estate
Tom and Megan McCleary

Our family of sponsors

Potash Brother's Supermart
Crate and Barrel
FAO Schwarz

Special Thanks

Margie Geddes, Mrs. Red Stripe
Vivian Valguarnera, Retail Banking Officer
Gary Pett, President and CEO, Cosmopolitan
    Bank and Trust
O. Mikki Van Winkle-Vice President
Daniel Watts, President and CEO,
    Pullman Bank and Trust Company
Louise Hilderbrand, Senior V. P. Trust Officer
Daniel J. Fumagalli, Esq.
Joshua Sidney Hyman, Esq.
Mark Logan, Esq.
Ballantyne Cashmere
Harpo Productions, Oprah.Com
O Magazine

J&L Foods Inc., Caterer
Unity in Chicago, Reverend Ed Townley
Gary Zukav
Eric Copage
Connie Eyer – Personal Assistant to Reverend Ed
Andre Walker
Ashby Stiff
Dorothy Clifford
Palmer Gene Smith, Sr., and Gene, Jr.
Lagran Saunders
Ben Baldwin
Jerry Kleiner
Lucini Italia
Susan Weaver
PJ Gray
Jeffrey Pawlak
Ina's
Senator and Mrs. Bob Graham
Robert Neubert
Dr. Eric Scheiber, M.D.

*Many thanks to our friends who contributed recipes so
this book could be as culturally diverse as our country.*

Rick Rodgers
Wilbert Jones
Ann Bloomstrand
Seth Roth
Diane Silverman
Nydia Cahue
Paula Golden
Mary Clay
Consuelo Arroyo
Nabila Ahmed
Naushab Ahmed
Evelyn Smith
Fredda Hyman
Mabel Jones
Addie Mae Smith
Adelaide Suber
Annella Schomburger
Katrina Markoff
Julie Lang
Karen Armijo
Domenica Catelli

Sources

Bradley's Country Store
10655 Centerville Road
Tallahassee, Florida 32308
(805) 893-1647
www.bradleycountrystore.com

Stone ground cornmeal, grits, cane syrup, and home-made country sausages.

Bridge Kitchenware Corp.
214 East 52nd Street
New York, New York 10022
(212) 838-6746, catalogue orders
www.bridgekitchenware.com

Comprehensive cookware, baking, and pastry supplies.

Crate and Barrel
646 North Michigan Avenue
Chicago, Illinois 60611
(800) 323-3461
www.crateandbarrel.com

Furnishings and home accessories.

Kalustyan's
123 Lexington Avenue
New York, New York 10016
(212) 685-3451

Sherry vinegar, Indian spices (black onion seeds, black mustard seeds, and black cumin seeds), and Asian ingredients (star anise, sweet chile sauce, canned coconut milk, and more).

Kitchen Food Shop
218 Eighth Avenue
New York, New York 10011
(212) 243-4433
www.kitchenmarket.com

Mexican ingredients, such as chiles de arbol, ground ancho and chipotle chile powders, masa harina, and dried corn husks.

Lucini Italia
Via Giulia 5-57020
Bolgheri, Tuscany, Italy
(888) 558-2464
www.lucini.com

Extra virgin olive oil, gran riserva balsamico, pinot grigio vinegar.

Martha White Flour
200 Butler Drive
Murfreesboro, Tennessee 37133
(800) 663-6317
www.marthawhite.com

Self-rising flour.

The Mustard Museum
100 West Main Street
Mount Horeb, Wisconsin 53572
(800) 438-6878
www.mustardmuseum.com

Laurent de Clos Watercress Mustard, Laurent de Clos Walnut Mustard, and Cuisine Perel Late Harvest Riesling Vinegar.

Oriental Pantry
423 Great Road
Acton, Massachusetts 01720
(978) 264-4576
www.orientalpantry.com

Asian ingredients, such as sweet chile sauce (from Singapore), canned coconut milk, star anise, hoisin sauce, rice vinegar, and dark Asian sesame oil.

Vosges Haut-Chocolat
2105 West Armitage
Chicago, Illinois 60647
(888) 301-YUMM
www.vosgeschocolate.com

Vosges Haut-Chocolat Aztec Elixir Cocoa, truffles.

Index